Gift of

MENLO MOTHERS' CLUB

SOUTINE

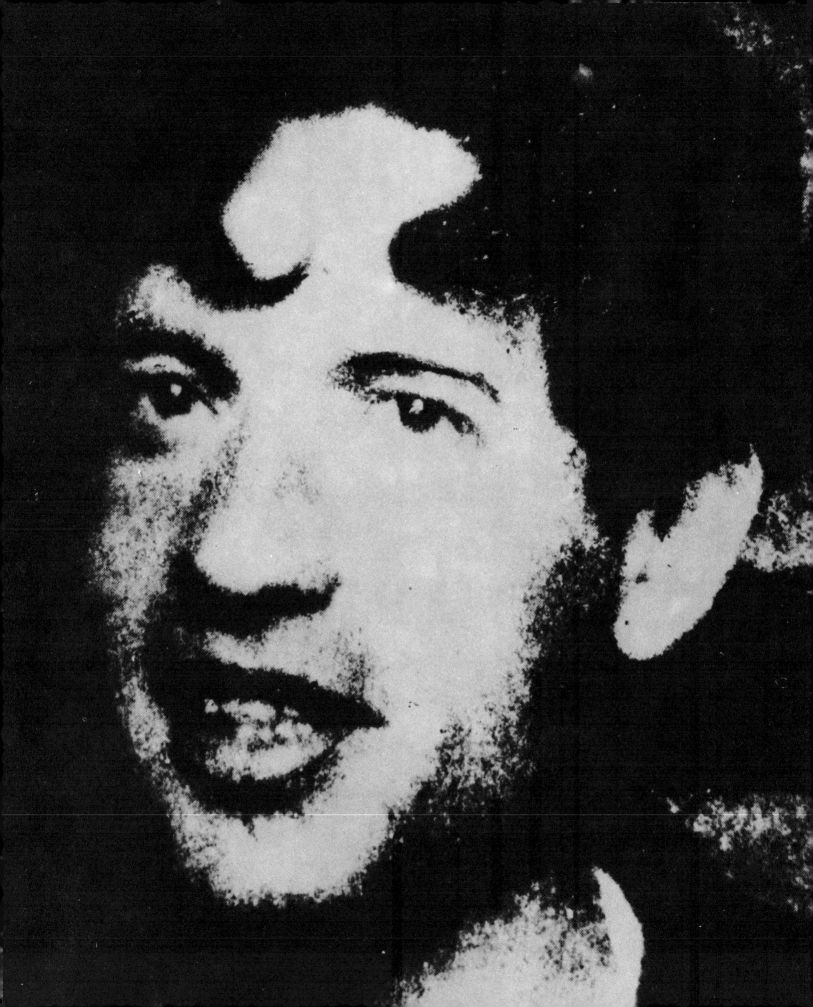

SPRING ART BOOKS

BY ANDREW FORGE

SPRING BOOKS · LONDON

ACKNOWLEDGMENTS

The paintings in this volume are reproduced by kind permission of the following collections and galleries to which they belong: Albright—Knox Art Gallery, Buffalo, N.Y. (Plate 28); The Ben Uri Art Gallery, London (Plate 6); Dr and Mrs Harry Bakwin, New York (Plate 21); M. and Mme Marcellin Castaing, Lèves, Eure-et-Loire (Plates 34, 42); Mr and Mrs Ralph F. Colin, New York (Plates 7, 20, 38, 41; Plate 41 is the property of Pamela T. Colin; Fogg Art Museum, Harvard University, Mass. — Gift of Mr and Mrs Ralph F. Colin (Plate 11); Mr and Mrs Matthew H. Futter, New York (Plate 3); Miss Adelaide Milton de Groot, New York (Plates 4, 35); M. Jacques Guérin, Paris (Plate 44); M. Georges Halphen, France (Plate 36); Kunstmuseum, Lucerne (Plate 37); Mr and Mrs Irving Levick, Buffalo, N.Y. (Plate 1); M. Pierre Lévy, Troyes (Plates 19, 23, 26, 31); Mr and Mrs Albert A. List, New York (Plate 17); Alex Maguy, Galerie de l'Elysée, Paris (Plate 48); Marlborough Fine Art Ltd., London (Plate 22); McRoberts and Tunnard Ltd., London (Plate 2); Musée National d'Art Moderne, Paris (Plate 32); Rex de C. Nan Kivell, Esq., London (Plate 18); Mr and Mrs Henry Pearlman, New York (Plate 5); The Henry Pearlman Foundation, New York (Plates 9, 14, 15); Perls Galleries, New York (Plates 8, 13, 16); Phillips Collection, Washington, D.C. (Plates 43, 45); Jack and Lillian Poses, New York (Plate 27); Alex Reid and Lefevre Ltd., London (Plate 39); Baronne Alix de Rothschild, Paris (Plate 33); E & A Silberman Galleries, New York (Plate 10); The Trustees of the Tate Gallery London (Plate 12); George Waechter Memorial Foundation, Geneva (Plate 25); Mme Jean Walter, Paris (Plate 24); M. Pierre Wertheimer, Paris (Plates 30, 47); Mrs L.B. Westcott, Rosemont, New Jersey (Plate 40): Mr Richard S. Zeisler, New York (Plate 29). The black and white photographs in this volume are reproduced by kind permission of: Musée du Louvre, Paris (Figures 1, 6); Nolde Foundation, Seebüll (Figure 7); Rijksmuseum, Amsterdam (Figure 2); Solomon R. Guggenheim Museum (Figures 3, 4); São Paulo Museum, Brazil (Figure 5).

The following photographs were supplied by: Clichés des Musées Nationaux (Figures 1, 7); Michael Holford, London (Plates 1—18, 20—30, 33—48); Photographie Giraudon, Paris (Plate 32); Jacqueline Hyde, Paris (Plates 19, 31); Roger-Viollet, Paris (Frontispiece); Jean Roubier, Paris (Figure 8). All plates and figures 3 and 5 are © S. P. A. D. E. M., Paris, 1965, figure 4 is © A. D. A. G. P., Paris, 1965.

The publishers gratefully acknowledge permission to quote copyright passages in this book from the following:
The Arts Council of Great Britain; T. & T. Clark, Edinburgh 2 and Charles Scribners & Sons, New York 17; The Museum of Modern Art, New York; Penguin Books Ltd., Harmondsworth, Middlesex; Mr David Sylvester; Mr Maurice Tuchman; The Viking Press New York.

First published 1965
2nd Impression 1966
Published by

SPRING BOOKS

Drury House ● Russell Street ● London WC2
© Paul Hamlyn Ltd 1965
Printed in Czechoslovakia by Svoboda, Prague
T 1750

CONTENTS

BLACK AND WHITE ILLUSTRATIONS

INTRODUCTION

Nineteenth-century Russia treated its Jewish population as a hated parasite. Anti-semitism was built into the Russian legal system. Jews were subject to arbitrary laws which deprived them of the rights of property, of their own institutions, of their own identity. They lived under a constant threat of conscription, deportation or punitive taxation. Only a few jobs were open to them. They could only live in certain areas on the fringes of Russia itself. One of these areas was the 'Pale of Settlement', the provinces that ran along Russia's western boundary from the Baltic to the Black Sea. The Pale was a vast rural ghetto, the scene of an immeasurable misery which reached its climax with the promulgation of the so-called May Laws of 1882. It was from this feardrenched background that Soutine emerged to follow his arbitrary and mysterious desire to paint.

Smilovitchi, the Lithuanian village where he was born the tenth son of the village tailor, was absolutely without culture. The very thought of painting pictures was heretical in such an orthodox community, and from the first Soutine was made to know that he was sinning: 'Thou shalt not make unto thee any graven image or any likeness of anything that is in heaven above or that is in the earth beneath or that is in the water under the earth.' His struggle to find ways of breaking the Second Commandment is part of his legend: he stole from the household to buy a coloured pencil and was locked up in the cellar as punishment; he made a drawing of the village idiot, then asked the rabbi to pose for him. The aftermath reads like a parable: the rabbi's son beat him up severely, the rabbi paid Soutine's mother damages and with the money he was able to leave Smilovitchi to study at art school.

He was at the academy at Vilna for three years; then, in 1913, with the help of a doctor who had taken an interest in him, he left Lithuania for France. Once in Paris he enrolled at the École des Beaux Arts, joining the Atelier Cormon where years before Emile Bernard and Van Gogh had studied. He did not stay long but soon installed himself in the famous studio block called *La Ruche* (the Beehive) in the Impasse Dantzig moving not long afterwards to a studio in the Cité Falguière. Although he is said not to have been particularly sociable it is clear that within a short space of time he was in touch with advanced circles: Chagall and Kisling were friendly with Picasso, Apollinaire, Cendrars; Léger had a studio in *La Ruche*, so did Modigliani.

Modigliani became a close friend. Soutine sat for him twice. There can hardly have been a greater contrast between them: Modigliani, handsome, profoundly cultured, his modernity tinctured with Italian sweetness — Soutine uncouth, persecuted, learning every inch of the way, indifferent to the purely aesthetic statement. As the years went on Modigliani's self-destructive drinking and drug-taking became more and more an end in itself. He found it harder to work, he was dying of consumption. Just as Soutine must surely have learned from his culture, so he may also have been hardened by Modigliani's personal failure. His own attachment to his work was fanatical, anxious. Although he appears to have suffered from periods of terrible sterility, he did not dodge them, but sweated them out, exploring every nuance of doubt and despair. He had stomach ulcers, the classic symptom of inner suffering, as David Sylvester has remarked.

Modigliani introduced Soutine to his dealer, the Polish poet Zborowski. By 1919 Zborowski had begun to help him and in that year he provided for him to leave Paris for Céret, the village in the Pyrenees where a number of artists, notably Picasso, Gris and Kisling, had worked for several summers before the war. Soutine was to work at Céret for the next four years and it was here that he was to paint what were among the most original paintings of the twentieth century.

An artist's work can be approached from two alternative directions: we can stress its place in the context of other art, as innovation, as a contribution to the dialectic of style — or we can see it as an isolated personal achievement. The first view leads us to reflect on the condition of art at the time; the second leads us to reflect on the content of the pictures themselves and their specific nature. Seen from the broader point of view a work of originality seems to propose a new definition of art; more narrowly it suggests an unprecedented testing of the self. We naturally approach an artist's earlier work in terms of its orientation, and the work of his maturity in terms of its inward nature, as though we imagine an artist taking up a stance in relation to his peers, and then turning to discover the implications of this stance, to find what it means to live it out.

It is remarkably difficult to apply these two perspectives to Soutine. It can't be denied that his earlier work, above all the landscapes painted at Céret, contains innovations which give it a unique place in twentieth-century painting. But it is difficult to place these innovations with any precision in the context of the art of the time. And yet it is not as though Soutine was an isolated figure — he was much less isolated than Chagall for instance, for all Chagall's Parisian air — on the contrary, he was a complex and, in a way, a sophisticated painter of outstanding technical fluency. But he cannot be convincingly related to any movement or manifesto of his time. We find ourselves looking at *all* his work in terms of its inner necessity, even while we analyse the formal changes that it underwent, and even while we recognise its debt to other painting.

1. Van Gogh, *Self-portrait*. 1890.

2. Rembrandt, *The Jewish Bride*. About 1658.

3. Léger, *Smokers*. 1911.

4. Delaunay, *Eiffel Tower*. 1914.

His art is supremely personal. He seems to be painting as we look. His pictures seem to be saturated by his presence, to reek of him.

I see Soutine's arrival in Paris as a fantastic conjunction. From nothing, a cultural desert, he finds himself in the Louvre, facing Rembrandt, Corot, Courbet, the skill and taste and sumptuousness of centuries. From a closed rural society he finds himself in an open culture at the climax of half a century of ferment. It is a measure of his stamina and the force of his need for self-definition that he was able to absorb and use so much. Of course Paris met him half way. Art itself was in a crisis of self-definition. Style couldn't be described any more in unified terms, only in personal ones, or utopian ones. The cultural mass was splitting up. 'A new emphasis lay on the character and act of the performance behind the work', as Adrian Stokes has reminded us, 'because art seemed to be creating culture rather than culture art: the individual's, the artist's achievement with himself could appear to be more stable than society's achievement'. Thus Soutine's reading of art was as valid as anyone's; in pulling himself up by his own boot straps he had, if anything, an advantage, not a disadvantage, in relation to his Western colleagues. If Paris had been stable, Soutine would have remained an outsider. But just as the dispossessed emigrant in America is in a sense more free to define himself as an American (as well as under greater pressure to do so) than a more fortunate and better-rooted one, so it was here: the Paris of Guillaume Apollinaire was an America of the mind.

We know nothing of what Soutine did as a student at Vilna, but we can guess from the evidence of his earliest surviving pictures that he would have been taught the dark tonal naturalism which was until so recently the universal language of the academies. These early pictures such as the *Studio at the Cité Falguière*, the *Still-life with Soup Tureen* (reproduced on pages 32 and 36 in *Soutine* by Monroe Wheeler) or the *Still-life with Lemons* (plate 1) are in essentials remarkably consistent with the work of his maturity, although they are full of hesitations and crudities and the handling is immature and sometimes strained. But all the hallmarks of his vision are here: the character of the image that convinces us that the subject was before his eyes when he painted it; the vitality with which the forms are described; the expressive deformation in the drawing. These elements are hardly to be separated. They are integral to his vision. Nothing is to change here as the years go by, nothing drops out. Only at certain times and in individual pictures one or another of these aspects will perhaps come to the fore. He will become more skilful, certainly, and above all his handling will become more free. But all that this means is that his relationship with the paint itself becomes subsumed more fully in his relationship with the things he is painting.

It is impossible to say how much Soutine knew of modern art before he came to Paris. It seems unlikely that he would have come into direct contact with any aspect of it in Vilna; but that is not to say that he would have been completely ignorant of it.

Lithuania was part of Russia and there must have been some echoes in Vilna of the artistic ferment of pre-war Moscow; he could have seen the magazine *Apollon* for instance. It seems even more likely that he would have been aware of current tendencies in Germany, for Jewish culture tended to be oriented towards Germany. If he had seen *Pan*, or *Die Insel* or *Der Sturm* as seems quite likely he would not only have known of Van Gogh and Cézanne, Matisse and Picasso, but also of the artists of *Die Brücke* of whom both Kirchner and Heckel might well have stirred him. At any rate the principle of expressive deformation would not have been unknown to him before he reached Paris.

Once in Paris the interesting thing is that he does not appear to have hesitated for a moment. This is striking when one considers the multiplicity of directions in which painters were thrusting — the very painters with whom he was mixing — and the inevitable difficulties and anxieties that must have crowded in on him at this time. But he doesn't seem to have experimented, or to have faltered in his stance.

What this stance amounted to was first of all a total commitment to direct painting from nature — and a consequent rejection of all the synthetic aspects of modern art.

Ever since the 1880s the main line of artistic thought had been a kind of criticism of realism, of impressionism, of *plein airism* — that is, of the whole naturalistic tradition of the nineteenth century. One wing of this criticism, descending from Gauguin, had been concerned with a dematerialised expression, an art of mood, of symbol, of states of mind; another, descending from Seurat and Cézanne and Van Gogh had concerned itself with confronting appearances with the reality of the picture, and with questioning the formal as well as the representative possibilities of the picture. What was common to all these efforts was that they started from an analysis of pictorial means. This was obviously the case with artists who rejected 'painting from nature' in favour of a more inventive approach; it was no less so with a painter like Bonnard who, while retaining the Impressionist language, synthesised it from memory rather than face to face with his model, or with a painter like Matisse who tended to work to the limits of abstraction, but with the model in front of him. 'When difficulties stopped me in my work', Matisse says in Apollinaire's famous interview, 'I said to myself: I have colours, a canvas, and I must express myself with purity, even though I do it in the briefest manner by putting down, for instance, four or five spots of colour or by drawing four or five lines which have a plastic expression.'

This standing back from the means of expression as though from a self-sufficient keyboard is fundamental to the development of modern art. In rejecting the descriptive role in painting it is also rejecting the muddle of appearances, the vague, streaming quality of visual impressions. It puts observation, response, the complexity of nature at a discount, and makes every claim on invention and constructive simplification. Description is ousted by metaphor; observation by invention. All this amounts to the outlining of a new art in which the emotional centre is located in the picture itself, its surface, its nature as an organism; and by implication it dismisses the old art in which the emotional centre is in what is represented.

Soutine was in no doubt as to where he belonged. He identified himself wholeheartedly with the tradition of painting in front of appearances. For him contact with the subject was an emotional necessity. And nowhere in his work is there the least hint of the kind of formalistic experiment or technical perfectionism that is implicit in all the synthetic art of his time. We feel that to him painting was a far more direct activity. He was close up to the sensations of seeing, feeling, experiencing. No process of analysis and synthesis mediated between the experience and the picture as it does in, for example, Bonnard and Matisse. For him painting is an inspired muddle, a sort of wrestling with experience rather than a standing back from it or an extended transformation of it. He was, in fact like a nineteenth-century painter, a realist, except that for him this was a brand new thing, rather than the culmination of a long tradition.

This is perhaps why he is said always to have professed indifference to Van Gogh, the one artist who, at this distance, seems to have given him the most. If one compares Soutine's first important painting, the *Self-portrait* (plate 5) of about 1918, with a Van Gogh *Self-portrait* (figure 1), one sees that every accent in the Van Gogh seems to reflect an act of conscious definition, like a word. The picture opens itself to us through its drawing. The drawing of the Soutine, on the other hand, is inscrutable. One has the feeling that it *happened*. It is impossible to imagine Soutine unravelling a particular knot, making an explication to himself of a particular problem. It is not that the painting looks more spontaneous (there could hardly be more life than in the Van Gogh head) but that it looks more unpredictable. Van Gogh, one imagines, really wanted to master his picture, to be able to say to himself that the picture mirrored such and such an intention: hence its completed quality, as of a journey done. The Soutine makes us wonder why he put it aside. Its pulsations are of a different order: the head could swell and swallow up the canvas, the tie could fly off. There is an absence of logic in the curious shape of the collar and the shoulder of his jacket — at least it seems so as long as we try to refer it to the rest of the jacket. But as soon as we stop doing this and see it as a phenomenon on its own, we see how like the loop of the right ear the collar is and how like the line of the cheek the shoulder is. We begin to recognise a kind of convulsiveness in the drawing against which the particulars of the head are just holding their own.

It is perhaps at this point that Soutine's affinities with Van Gogh can be defined. All self-portraits are more than likenesses. There is an element of introspection in them, of self-characterisation: one thinks of Courbet's heroic posturing, or the gamut of expressions that Cézanne explored in the late 'sixties. But what is special to Van Gogh, and distinguishes him from any painter before, is that he is not painting himself in order to paint a certain kind of picture. The 'kind of picture' is identified with its subject, the painter. For all its self-conscious structure it is impossible to imagine the resolution of this picture applied to different circumstances. What the picture is about and how it happened are one and the same. The implication is that the picture comes directly out of sensation, that sensation preceded the pictorial intention. Whatever ideas he may have had about painting, the nature of pictures, or art, are subsumed in the primary experience of the subject. The subject is recognised as meaningful in its own right, and also in its relationship to the painter and in its function as a focus to his attention. For the time being the painter is part of it, his affections, aggressions, fears, needs, are flowing out to it and being answered by it. The self-portrait is a self-portrait in more senses than that of likeness: for a landscape by Van Gogh or a still-life is also a self-portrait. This could hardly be said of an Impressionist, for however empirical the Impressionists thought they were being, there was an intention behind all their work which was both descriptive and aesthetic. To this extent there is a wider gap between them and their subject — the subject is less important in itself and it is chosen for its visible qualities rather than for the resonance it has in the mind and imagination of the painter. For Van Gogh the subject was of profound autobiographical importance on every level. I do not mean simply in its function as parable — the Sower as Life, the Reaper as Death — but in its every aspect, as though by articulating his experience of a part of the world he was unifying his experience of the whole world, giving form to his relation to it.

Soutine, then, having nothing to do with the rationalism of Van Gogh's technique, has everything to do with his understanding of content. His posture is more extreme; his subjectivity far more ruthless and consuming. He could afford this if only because he was painting pictures that were on the face of it *less* extreme than others that were being painted at the same time.

It is in terms of this totally engrossed, primitive relationship to the painting act, in which he seems to demand something of it rather than to make something with it, that we can best understand Soutine. As I have said, in later years he disclaimed Van Gogh. He was clearly aware of and in a certain idiosyncratic way influenced by Cézanne and Bonnard. But he gave his unreserved admiration to pre-Impressionist artists, to Tintoretto and El Greco at first, later to Rembrandt, Courbet and Corot. Soutine's admiration for Rembrandt led him once to sit up for two nights in the train so that he could spend a whole day at the Rijksmuseum in front of the *Jewish Bride* (figure 2). There are two instances of his having painted subjects which were reconstructed from works by Rembrandt: the *Carcass* of 1925 and the *Woman Bathing* which he painted in 1929 and again in 1931 (see plates 28 and 34). He did the same with Courbet. There is, for example, a *Siesta* in the Castaing collection which is reconstructed from a study for *Les Demoiselles Aux Bords de la Seine*; and a *Salmon*, also in the Castaing collection, is a tribute to Courbet's treatment of the same subject.

These influences were to become increasingly important to him as he grew older. In the present context it is obvious that what Rembrandt and Courbet have in common

14

is an unreserved grip of material actuality. Forget the 'grandeur' of Rembrandt, the dramatic *mise en scène*, and one is left with a solidity, sometimes clayey, sometimes brassy, always tough, dense, and so actual that it is like a rediscovery of matter. Solidity seems to be apprehended on such a primary level that one hardly knows by what sense or organ one receives it: through one's eyes or under the palm of one's hand or against the roof of one's mouth. Of course it is with these powerful and disturbing sensations that Rembrandt structures a whole world. This is his measure, that his architecture is as ambitious as his material is earthy. We find our extremes in him, infants called to respond to the most ambitious constructions while still uninhibitedly muck-raking. It was surely this double value in his work that meant most to Soutine, the fact that his enormous spiritual strength was founded on a response to the undifferentiated materiality of things. It was surely in Rembrandt's encrusted surfaces and the phenomenal quality of his forms that Soutine found the strongest symbol of his own experience in front of nature. For Rembrandt's surfaces hardly ever distance themselves, or even easily identify themselves: can we say we even *see* them rather than knead them or rake them or comb them as though they were part of ourselves?

Rembrandt's structure means nothing to him. Soutine wants no part of the architecture of art; he can, or will accept nothing of its cultural implications, those mature imperatives to balance and order that constitute the outward message of the old masters (that message that Van Gogh fought desperately to re-create within his own sensations). Was it that Soutine was debarred from these structures by his origins, primitive in western terms? Or was it simply that in him we are recognising an aspect of modern art, which involves a kind of regression, an orientation of personality that has no place for sensation *and* order? Both, probably — the two interlock. It is impossible to imagine that Soutine would have found any place or any voice as an artist at any time but our own.

In one of the first pictures painted at Céret (*Trees at Céret*, plate 6) the front of the canvas is quite filled by the gnarled forms of tree trunks. It is just possible to see between them to the buildings beyond. One feels fenced in by the monster trees — there is no escape into the distance — their dark, writhing trunks rake up and down the canvas and offer no release. It is a nightmarish picture, an image of panic and hysteria.

Soon Soutine was to eliminate the suggestion of depth which makes this picture so disquieting. *Landscape at Céret* (plate 12) provides hardly any sense of movement into the picture, but in return the surface rhythms are even wilder, more violent, more convoluted. Although he later turned his back on these pictures, rejecting their implications, they are among his most important works. They are certainly his most original from the stylistic point of view, and one can't help thinking that much of the content of his later work was first grasped at Céret. Two characteristics dominate these pictures: their violent all-over movement and their dense, compressed space. What were the origins of these qualities and what was specific about them?

Movement is such an essential part of Soutine's work that it is worth considering what one means by it as an attribute of painting. A picture can describe moving objects; it can also itself be organised in a dynamic or rhythmical way. The two do not necessarily coincide (Poussin painted still pictures of dancing figures, Rubens painted rhythmical pictures of stationary figures) but there is always the possibility of making them coincide. The painting of this century has been obsessed with both aspects of movement, that is with new ways of expressing movement on the part of the object (Balla's *Lady with a Dog*, Duchamp's *Nude Descending a Staircase*) and also with new ways of incorporating it into the structure of the picture (Klee: 'I should like to create an order from feeling and, going still further, from motion'). The two exemplars of this obsession are Van Gogh and Cézanne. Both saw that movement was a key bridge between the picture and what it was of, both found unexplored relationships between the rhythms of drawing and the rhythms of the things they drew. But their treatment of movement was quite distinct.

In a late landscape by Van Gogh everything in the picture seems to writhe or coil; nothing stands still. It is the *drawn* quality of the movement which matters: it is descriptive as well as aesthetic, a functional notation as well as an abstract one.

In Cézanne movement is far more complex. Movement, the sinuous flicker of his forms, was not descriptive, nor was it a stylistic rhythm with which the subject was made to dance. It was the tempo of his response to picture and subject alike, the mediating rhythm between the manifold impressions of out there and the single static fact of the canvas. The magnificent movements of *Le Grand Pin* (figure 5), shaggy, towering, serene, are Cézanne's movements, finalised under the circumstances of painting the tree.

The energy that flows through the work that Soutine did at Céret partakes of qualities that we find in both Van Gogh and Cézanne. The slippery, sliding curves of the early *Still-life with Fish* (plate 22) have a nearly caricatural intention; the jerky convulsions in the drawing of the *Self-portrait* (plate 5) are Soutine's convulsions and suggest an inward rhythm, finalised under the special circumstances of the subject. In the Céret landscapes everything moves. Outward characterisation of the scene and the painter's inner spasm are interlocked in an extraordinary fusion in which neither takes a dominant part.

In the *Landscape* (plate 12) it is not easy to tell what each paint stroke represents. We can see that the picture is of a sloping hillside with a red-roofed building on the left and a peak beyond. We can identify a tree, green bushes, a bit of sky. But this does no more than to give us the roughest orientation. Most of the time we are bumping about like a person stumbling over a ploughed field in the twilight, hardly knowing where our eye is leading us, dictated to by the violent ridges, checked by furrows

16

turned back on themselves. The house seems to be tilting at a disastrous angle. But how are we to interpret its tilt — as a caricature of foreshortening, or an expression of the precipitous fall of the hillside, or as something less easily related to physical phenomena? — for the longer we look at it the more it seems to shoot *up* the hill in a course parallel to the picture plane.

The fact is that the movements in this picture are no more to do with the inherent character of the subject than they are to do with the painter's reactions to the subject. We feel that a storm rages, the earth trembles out there; but we also feel as though a storm, an earthquake is being projected on to the landscape. Is its violence the violence of a high wind or the violence of the painter? These coiling greens along the upper edge of the picture could be coiling storm clouds, or just coiling paint, an expression of coilingness, a spasm in the paint.

These are extreme pictures which push the subjectivity of painting to an unprecedented point. And the most extreme instance is the *Hill at Céret* (plate 16). Never before and rarely since has painting taken on this immediacy or conveyed this sense of the painter's spasm locked into the paint. And yet while recognising this unique and original quality it would be a mistake to think of his achievement as something without a background. All painters work with available possibilities; originality may be measured in these terms. The total movement of the *Hill at Céret* is only possible because Soutine is working with a fragmented image: because, that is, particular paint marks are thought of as distinct from the wholeness of the objects that they represent. This in turn is possible because the flatness of the canvas is allowed to dominate the spatial depth of the subject. Both characteristics derive from Cubism.

As we have seen, Soutine showed no direct interest in the Cubist adventure. But he was by no means unaffected by it. Soutine's filled in, brimming canvases of this period are unthinkable without analytical Cubism. Compare his *Red Roofs, Céret* (plate 15), for example, with Léger's *The Smokers* (figure 3). Given the painterly immediacy of the one and the synthetic reserve of the other, one is struck by the many agreements between them. There is the same shallow, dense space. Perspective is contradicted in the architecture so that no vanishing points are allowed to pierce into depth. The problem of the sky is handled similarly in both pictures by raking forms across the upper corners of the canvas, closing them off. Both painters carry a vertical up the front of the canvas — the tree on the left of the Soutine, and on the left of the Léger an alignment of tube-like forms, confirming and consolidating the picture surface.

A further comparison with the pre-1914 *avant garde* can be made. The most satisfactory model for the Céret landscapes seems to me to be provided by the pictures which Delaunay painted in 1910 of the Eiffel Tower. It was of these that Apollinaire said that they were like pictures of an earthquake, something that must have been said thousands of times since about Soutine. But again the spirit is completely different — Delaunay's gaiety against Soutine's dark absorption. Delaunay's *Eiffel Tower* (figure 4) is the first picture in which pictorial movement is carried to such an extreme point that the buildings appear to dance; or to look at it another way, the first painting in which Cubist distortion is carried to such a point that you cannot tell whether movement is to be attributed to the building or to the kinetics of the picture.

After 1923 a marked change comes over Soutine's approach. This coincides with a change in his fortunes following his discovery by the American collector Barnes. His reputation established, and free from want, he left Céret and returned to Paris, spending periods at Cagnes on the Riviera. The change in his work amounted to a rejection of many of the most original features of his Céret pictures, and a return of a sort to the structure of his early pictures. But his mastery of the medium was now complete; indeed, one of the most striking features of the change is the sudden emergence of a calligraphic virtuosity in his handling which is not foreshadowed anywhere in his earlier work. From this point onwards he appears to close his eyes completely to modern painting while at the same time pushing his own idiosyncratic vision to more extreme lengths.

As we have seen when looking at the Céret pictures, their extraordinary energy is linked with the way in which space is flattened and compressed. What happens now is that he begins to open the space out in his pictures, to allow for distance and perspective. This development is accompanied by a far greater attachment to the identity of the things he is painting: houses become definitely houses, roads more than just directional bars of paint. The emphasis on movement does not slacken but now the movement in the picture looks like an *animation* of the thing painted.

The picture *Houses at Cagnes* (plate 25) was painted only a couple of years after *Hill at Céret* (plate 16), yet it seems a life-time away in its mood and structure. Forms are whole and clear-cut. They interlock according to a wayward but quite intelligible logic. Indeed, the picture functions like a rustic version of a classical composition, with its interleaving masses of houses and hills and sky. What in the Céret pictures was primarily an expression of movement in the paint reads here as distortion. Walls lean or sag, nod from side to side. Reminiscences of the whirlpool oblivion of Céret cling to the foreground, the strangely uprooted foliage on the left, and particularly to the buried clambering figure in the turn of the road; but once past the immediate foreground, the intention is towards clarity.

It is clarity of a strange kind: there is a suggestion of folklore and fairy-tale, of crooked doors and crooked roofs, winding steps and little crooked men. These pictures have been likened to Disney, not without reason. The best known instance is a landscape in the Castaing collection, much reproduced, in which white houses seem to dance and fly in a pale blue air and his brush plays across the canvas with an almost oriental delicacy.

This calligraphic gesturing with the brush, which first appears so unexpectedly in

18

5. Cézanne, *Le Grand Pin*. 1892—96

6. Courbet, *Funeral at Ornans* (detail). 1850.

7. Nolde, *The Matterhorn Smiles*. 1894.

8. The West Front of Chartres Cathedral

the Cagnes pictures, was to become an increasingly important element. As it got more free and inventive it became the medium by which movement is carried to new extremes. By making a representational spatial structure he projects his obsession with movement outwards on to the landscape: the violent movements of his brush take up what I have called his inner movements. The two tendencies arrive at a remarkable equilibrium in the last great pictures of trees so that one can hardly say what is to be attributed to the painting and what to the subject.

In these pictures, perspective plays an important part in the image. There is never doubt as to what is what. Changes of scale operate as in a traditional picture. Violent movement runs through the whole canvas, stemming both from the tossing forms of the trees and from the enormous vigour and the varieties of gesture that animate the paint. These pictures are both more airy and more particularised than the Céret landscapes, but they have much of the intensity of the earlier works and much of their formal freedom. Two factors would seem to contribute to this freedom, this total expressive vitality of the picture surface. Firstly the subject itself. The trees present an eloquent surface, reared up against the picture plane, closing it effectively from perspective. They are themselves closed, brimming forms, analogues for the canvas, filled with nothing but tossing movements, vehicles for wind and weather no less than for the spontaneous discharges of his brush. They make his gestures just as they seem to make their own. Secondly, it is noticeable that Soutine goes to lengths to to relate these trees to the rectangle of the canvas. He brings them square into the field of the canvas — a row of them facing it closely, or if in an avenue, locked together in a great squarish arch that crams the canvas. Furthermore he seizes on every clue to bring their verticality into relation with the surface of the canvas — as in the Phillips Collection *Windy Day, Auxerre,* (plate 45), where the path in the foreground is linked with the crack of the sky between the trees, and the leaning trees on the left are drawn into a continuous form with the sky by the diagonal of cloud that cuts the corner of the canvas.

So far I have discussed the formal characteristics of Soutine's painting without questioning its relevance to content. Yet Soutine is of course a painter to whom content was everything. The point hardly needs stressing: he is like a person who is incapable of uttering a word lightly or in a flat or neutral tone. His art is passionate, temperamental, extreme. It seems to mirror a solitary experience, to have been suffered to a degree that is without parallel even in the art of our century. We feel this to be so not merely on the grounds of his subject-matter — the anxiety-ridden features of his sitters or the aura of death that clings to his still-lifes — but also in the structure of the paint and the composition of his pictures. His work seems to realise more fully than any other Zola's demand for 'a man and not a picture', for 'a bit of creation seen through the medium of a powerful temperament'.

Even when Zola wrote this famous phrase, there was nothing new about it. The idea that a work of art reflects the personality of its maker goes back to antiquity, but it was not until the nineteenth century that it became a central preoccupation. With much of twentieth-century art, and above all with the art that is lumped together under the heading of Expressionism it is a *sine qua non*, the ultimate substitute for an aesthetic.

Soutine's name is surrounded by legends. There are stories of his poverty, his paranoia, his fanaticism, his selfishness, his dedication, his anguish. Most of them, as David Sylvester has pointed out, revolve round his passionate and quasi-religious devotion to the motif. Others, hardly less startling, dramatise his ecstatic concentration while painting. Inevitably anyone who knows these stories brings them to his reading of the pictures. But of course the only *artistic* significance the stories have is that they are told about the author of the pictures, not the other way round.

Although Soutine painted directly from nature, he did not, as the Impressionists had done, work in the spirit that any piece of nature was almost as good as any other to paint, and that what counted was not what it was in itself but the aesthetic impressions that could be gained from it. For him it mattered desperately where he was or what he painted. His friends would drive him for miles and days in search of the right model or the right motif. Once he had found what he wanted, he worked with such fervour and concentration that he lost all sense of time and place and even on one occasion, the story goes, injured himself painting without knowing how he did it.

This fanatical particularity passes directly into the pictures. His figures are so individual as to be monstrous. And this is in spite of the extremely narrow range of pose and type, and the repetitive mannerisms which almost invariably mark his treatment of certain features. It is not possible to relate his subjects to a general intention outside the painting experience. He wasn't like a Daumier or a Van Gogh whose subjects can be seen to add up to a view of the world. His sitters are of all types: when he was young they were his friends, and peasants at Céret. Later they are bourgeois. Nothing of a social nature can be deduced from his famous series of uniformed figures, the cooks and choir-boys and bellhops of the late 'twenties. Only at the end of his life is there a suggestion of his figures standing for something. The little figures that scurry in his late landscapes can perhaps be read symbolically, as can also a late painting called *Maternité* in the Castaing collection, in which a woman sits with a sleeping or dead child in her lap. But these are the exceptions.

All that his figures have in common from first to last is their singularity. He seems to look at them as if at freaks — as if appalled by the differentness of human beings. There seems to be no limit to the strangeness that he finds in them: look for instance at the *Woman in Red* (plate 21), one of his greatest pictures, at the incredible asymmetry of hat and face and pose, at the weird reversals of the features, the grotesque quality of the woman's milky-pink skin set against the poppy-red of her dress.

22

It is the same with his still-lifes. We do not feel, as we do with Van Gogh, that his groups are arranged as if to enact a parable. Nor do we feel, as we do with Cézanne, that the configuration of objects is an architectonic structure, a demanding composition out there on the table-top. His arrangements circle round certain themes connected with food and with death, this is true. But what carries these themes is his obsessive awareness of the individual pieces or objects out of which the group is made. A painter may look at a tomato as a patch of red, or as a sphere flattened in a particular way, or as a metaphor, a jewel, a drop of blood. For Soutine it was first a tomato — and a miracle, a grotesque and marvellous event that it should look like one, or so he makes us feel. His fish, like his sitters, are monsters — his dead turkeys are fabulous even when they are most turkey-like. The last thing that he could ever do was to see a still-life as an harmonious arrangement. His pictures are rarely what painters call 'in tone': certain colours always obtrude; the surface is rarely a unified whole.

The question remains how these feelings are communicated in his pictures — for Soutine's pictures do communicate in a uniquely vivid way. The answer would seem to be contained in the quality of deformation which runs as a constant through everything he painted. Deformation, distortion — the words suggest a norm from which the painter is departing; a certain starting point at which the object is whole, intact, 'natural', and on the basis of which the painter proceeds to work his expressive changes. This is of course true of all original painting; development occurs against a background of 'normality'. We expect a picture to look a certain way and we react with anger or delight as an artist of originality modifies, distorts or outstrips our expectation. In a sense, whatever he says is phrased against our expectation as though against a sounding-board. This is the history of art. What is specific about Soutine's position is that the norm with which he was working was the norm of the nineteenth century: that is to say, naturalism. Before that, in the eighteenth century and earlier, the norm had been based on style; naturalism placed the idea of truth to nature, 'likeness', over and above style. Indeed it sees itself as an anti-style in which nature's authority replaces the authority of the studio. The onlooker's expectations of a naturalistic painting include his preconceptions of pictures and his preconceptions of natural appearances too. He is thus doubly sensitive, doubly exposed to the irritant of distortion.

Seen from this angle, Soutine's rejection of the Céret pictures is less mysterious. It may well be that, like Picasso and Braque at the height of analytical Cubism, he felt that the Céret pictures were simply too hard to read; and that he had to return to more literal appearances so that his *deformations could register*. It may be that he had to recover both a more stable norm of appearances and a more stable pictorial norm. Advanced art was dedicated to the destruction of all pictorial norms, but Soutine had special expressive urgencies. Courbet and Corot offered the last stable norm. Soutine told René Gimpel that what he liked about Courbet was that he was 'direct'; Corot gave him the same sensation of immediate contact with things.

Corot is particularly *à propos* in the present context — Corot who painted with a probably closer and more perfect sense of natural tone than any other painter; who brought natural observation and the traditions of classical composition into a more perfect alignment than any other painter; whose ultimate hallmarks were stillness, clarity, a steadfast and loving detachment. We may well imagine that it was against such a painter that Soutine twisted and turned, grappled his subject, destroyed it as he re-created it, fought it as he honoured it.

It was not always a generalised norm that he worked against either. Many times he carried his admiration for his favourite painters to the point of painting versions of their compositions, only from nature. Here he can build up a double pressure: he can exert pressure against his model by distorting or deviating from the composition of the original. He does this when he reverses the pose of the girl lying on her side in a picture called *The Siesta* in the Castaing collection, which is borrowed from Courbet's *Les Demoiselles aux bords de la Seine* or brings the wading woman into close-up in the pictures borrowed from Rembrandt's *Woman Bathing*. He can also work with the feeling that the scene in front of his eyes is also deviating from the original. The actuality of nature is opposed to the actuality of art as he paints. The raw particulars of nature are opposed to the formal particulars of art.

There is a further example of a rather different kind of his exploitation of a norm. This is his series of pictures of uniformed figures (plates 32, 33). The bright liveries set the sitters apart, make them exotic, anachronistic. But they also give Soutine a neutral base, a uniform literally against which to set the individual features of the sitter. Their effect is particularly clear when one sees two scarlet clad valets side by side. Then one can hardly doubt the importance to him of the common ground offered by the livery. Because, of course, the more circumscribed the subject, the more telling each variant of it becomes. It is interesting that at about the same time as Soutine began painting the uniformed figures, he also began to paint single dead animals and birds, repeating them in series. There are, for instance, a dozen canvases of hanging hares or rabbits. Repeated this way, the single form of the animal becomes like a code; every nuance is significant in a way that it would not be if the subject had not been painted under the same circumstances.

It is, of course, a fallacy to think of a 'norm' of appearances as something distinct from a particular historical expectation of a certain kind of picture. This is the misapprehension that painters laboured under for a hundred years. Naturalism is a style like any other, although it made claims to be beyond style. What matters particularly is that during the nineteenth century a new dimension was added to the painter's experience: I mean that which stems from the practice of painting directly from nature in the open air. The experience of painting from nature is something which was built in to the content of modern painting. No analogy exists in other arts for this experience. It provided painters with a range of relationships which they could not find in any other situation. (It could be argued that the highly specialised subjective nature of this experience did as much as anything to isolate painters from a public which could only interpret pictures through their imagery and not through the way they were painted.) At any rate, to work from nature is for many painters to feel that they are establishing a real contact with the outside world, and to feel that they are not only making something when they paint a picture but also handling something, or working with something that already exists. Appearances take on the quality of material, already formed but still to be absorbed, overcome, re-formed. Painting from nature is like a rehearsal, both imaginative and practical, of wider relationships with the outside world. To draw is also to handle; and by the same token to distort is to break or to attack, just as to organise is to command or to restore.

We know how important it was to Soutine to work from nature. And we can see how all through his work there is an excitement and an activity which leads us to think of his painting as a discharge of energy, a more or less strenuous response to whatever it is that forms and orders the thing in front of him. Gravity which makes a jug stand upright on the table in front of him is a force to be resisted, strained against; so too is the jug's symmetry. Pushing against it, deforming the jug, is paradoxically breaking it and confirming its symmetry, like a man biting his thumb to confirm his senses. The uprightness of the great trees is so unassailable that anything can be done with them, any tornado launched against them. Trees could hardly be more firmly rooted than his, nor twist more wildly against their roots. The symmetry of figures, of shoulders or the features of a face are the most potent configurations of all. They look back at him whatever he does to them. Indeed the more recklessly he improvises around them, the more magically they restore themselves and rekindle their vitality.

Soutine's painting of the façade of Chartres Cathedral (plate 40, figure 8) allows us to rehearse his process of deformation with some precision. There were many precedents for the subject; Monet and Pisarro at Rouen, Jongkind, Matisse and many others in front of Notre-Dame, Corot at Chartres itself. Soutine's cathedral differs from any of its predecessors first by its curious scale: he appears to have been at some distance from it since he includes the whole façade, yet the picture makes us feel that he is also very close up to it. There is certainly no suggestion in the painting of his having been guided, as Monet was for instance, by what could easily be taken in from one viewpoint. It seems rather to be a composite image built up from a multiplicity of impressions; and to be based more on a sense of the total phenomenon of the cathedral than on any particular visual aspect of it.

In this connection a statement by Monroe Wheeler is of particular interest: he tells us that twice during the painting Soutine enlarged it by roughly nailing new strips of wood to the original panel. 'It was a shortcoming of his talent', Wheeler adds, 'not knowing how to foresee the proportions of his subject matter within the dimensions of his board or canvas; there were often superfluities or insufficiencies.'

That the picture 'grew' as he painted it does not seem surprising when we notice how he transformed the architectural image. When Corot painted it he stressed the classical elements in the building, defining the main planes clearly, stressing the vertical and horizontal divisions and maintaining an impeccable hold of its areas and proportions. His building is all masonry with light falling across it. Soutine's building is closer to us in effect. It is literally closer in the way that it crams the canvas; it feels closer in the way in which he tends to ignore the divisions into which the building is ordered, thus making it more compact, more plastic, kneading it together. One notices that he has not allowed the balustrade above the rose window to make a continuous line with the top of the tower that carries the north spire; and that he has suppressed other horizontal elements. One notices also that he has exaggerated the batter of the south tower, and given it a long raking curve to which all the mouldings and window openings have to accommodate themselves, as if the tower itself was built of some tough, flexible material which was now being moulded and bent. He has given the tower a certain fullness too, a roundness that it doesn't possess in fact. The lacy detail of the north spire is bound into a single form, again as though he had compressed a tough but malleable material. The contrast with Corot here is particularly revealing: Corot slightly expands the same passage in the interests of clarity, so that he can reconstruct with the least loss of architectural coherence. But Soutine's spire, indeed his whole cathedral, is more like a living thing than a building, an organism which has grown, which palpitates and breathes and seems even to be facing us as we face it. Once we have seen it in this light it is difficult not to see the two spires as heads which stare back at us, or the piers as great stumpy legs resting on the ground. The whole configuration of the building, in fact, becomes personalised.

All writers on Soutine have noticed the way in which his subjects seem to have a life of their own, whether through their restless movements, or more specifically by their anthropomorphic suggestions. In *Fish and Tomatoes* (plate 27), for instance, the configuration of plate and forks suggests a head and grasping hands; a *Carcass of Beef* of 1926 in a private collection in Paris, suggests a lacerated head; many of the late tree paintings resolve themselves into waving limbs and staring eyes. Not that there is any evidence that Soutine deliberately sought these presences in the objects that he was painting: he could hardly have kept them at their mysterious subliminal level if this had been so. It is rather that in making his distortions from the norm he is led unavoidably to this situation, as though in broaching the conventional shell of the thing he is painting he is creating a vacuum which has to be filled by new presences. His objects are like mediums speaking with voices that come from who knows where.

Although transformations of this kind have been central to the formal as well as the expressive intentions of much of twentieth-century art, to Picasso, Klee, Sur-

26

realism, they play no part at all in the realist tradition of French painting to which Soutine had attached himself. The background to this aspect of his work is complex and calls for further examination.

Speaking of Soutine's great paintings of trees done at the end of his life, Monroe Wheeler comments that 'tree worship is a cult anciently established in the Lithuanian part of Russia. In Soutine's youth there were still arboreal rites in villages not far removed from Smilovitschi, and at the foot of any very noble specimen in the country-side one might find offerings. One can only conjecture whether he had this in mind years later.' Whether there is a connection here or not, this comment is a useful reminder of Soutine's background.

There is no question of his having made a virtue of his remote provincial origin, as Chagall did, for example. But, as we have already seen, there is a strong suggestion of folklore in the Cagnes landscapes (plates 17, 18, 19), a reminder that his background was not far removed from Chagall's. We may assume that he, too, was reared on tales of a similar kind, that his imagination was nurtured in a world where animals talked and trees walked and things took on the character of people. This is not necessarily to make a primitive out of him. Much of the advanced art that was being done in Russia before 1914 was involved in a rediscovery of folk art. Kandinsky, Goncharova, Male-vich and others had drawn on these sources, following a similar course to the Fauves and Cubists with their discovery of tribal sculpture. The same was true in Germany, where a good deal of folk-mysticism had actually been absorbed into the ideas of the advanced artists. German Expressionism had its origins in the cult of Nature. This was not at all the same thing as the 'truth to nature' of the Impressionists in France. It is the opposite of materialist, it implies a mystical approach to nature as a force; it implies a personalisation of nature's aspects. To this extent it implies a primitivistic attitude, an identification with the superstitions of primitive people, a heavily charged awareness of the subject's own response to nature, which is fostered and extended. Nature becomes not only an impelling force in its own right but also a living mirror for the observer's own emotional life. The two ideas are hardly distinguishable: the one grows out of the other.

There is a striking example of this in the early work of Emil Nolde (figure 7). The work which first made him known was a series of picture postcards done for the amusement of tourists, in which he represented famous mountains as heads, drawing on the names and legends that peasant traditions had woven round them. This person-alisation of nature was to lead directly into the expressionism of his later works where aspects of the natural world, the sea, a bunch of flowers, are painted as if to mirror the artist's inner state. 'Things are more than things when they are expressions of the soul', writes Otto Fischer, one of the theorists of Expressionism in Munich, and the phrase seems to contain the essence of the whole movement.

As we have seen above, there is no certainty about Soutine's knowledge of modern art before he came to Paris. The most we can say is that it would be strange if he had been completely ignorant of this view of subject-matter, just as it would be strange if such a neurotic and in many ways regressive character had been able to free himself completely of the superstitions of his peasant origins.

There is nothing overtly retrospective or nostalgic in Soutine's art. On the face of it he is a realist in the French tradition. But there is no denying that his view of the natural world is coloured with something very distant from the material hedonism of French art. He seems never to have painted anything as something removed from himself, at a distance. Everything he paints becomes part of himself. Another way of putting it is to say that he was never able to see a thing as an inanimate object removed from the world of living things or human feelings. Rather he endows everything with life, in the most literal sense. Even a dead bird becomes a living bird dying — or, dead only by the attention of a living observer. Either way it seems to be *enacting* or *suffering* its death.

A further speculation arises, one which touches on his Jewish background. Much has been written about the particular stresses that Soutine must have suffered as a result of his having broken away from an orthodox background in order to paint. Wheeler connects his almost religious dedication to art with this stress, suggesting that Soutine felt that he could atone for his apostasy only by the most complete self-sacrifice. Sylvester has related his traditionalism and his representational virtuosity to the same stress. The thought occurs that it is possible that having made this break he might well have searched, perhaps quite unconsciously, for a justifying attitude from within his own Jewish background with which to ennoble his activity as a painter. Such justification might have been found in the mystical teaching of the Hasidim.

Hasidism, the body of Jewish belief which grew up round the teaching of Ba'al Shem Tov in eighteenth-century Poland, had a considerable influence in the Pale of Settlement during the nineteenth century. It was pantheistic, mystical, anti-intellectual. Its teaching has most to say about man's relationship to the world: God is contained in all things and all people. There is nothing in creation which does not contain His presence. God's work is not done with; creation is a continuing process to which man by his attention to people and things makes a necessary contribution. The medium of contact with God is not the Law, or the analytical intellect, but a relationship, an ecstatic awareness of the world as it is.

Much of the content of Hasidism is contained in the work of the modern Jewish thinker Martin Buber who has stressed the distinction between the relation to the world expressed in the words *I-It* and that expressed in the words *I-Thou*. The I-It relationship involves experience, seeing people or things as outside phenomena contingent on other outside phenomena, with characteristics that can be listed, dissected, discussed. It involves a sense of distance between subject and object; it involves a sense of 'I' as a discrete entity. The I-Thou relationship is concerned with none of

28

these things; it is no more aware of the definable attributes of things than it is of the discrete limits of the observer. It is no more aware of the space that separates 'I' and 'Thou' than it is of categories into which either can be fitted. It is pure relation. Buber continually illustrates what he means by referring to primitive states, to infants or to primitive peoples: (*I and Thou*, English translation by R. G. Smith, Edinburgh, 1937).

'Consider the speech of "primitive" peoples, that is, of those that have a meagre stock of objects, and whose life is built up within a narrow circle of acts highly charged with presentness. The nuclei of this speech, words in the form of sentences and original pre-grammatical structures (which later, splitting asunder, give rise to the many various kinds of words), mostly indicate the wholeness of a relation. We say "far away"; the Zulu has for that a word which means in our sentence form, "There where someone cries out: 'O Mother I am lost.'" The Fuegian soars above our analytic wisdom with a seven-syllabled word whose precise meaning is "They stare at one another, each waiting for the other to volunteer to do what both wish, but are not able to do." In this total situation the persons, as expressed both in nouns and pronouns, are embedded, still only in relief and without finished independence. The chief concern is not with these products of analysis and reflection but with the true original unity, the lived relation.'

There is no doubt that Soutine's work suggests a comparable approach to the world. There is the same passionate involvement in things, the same sense that it is his attention, his state of relation which, as it were, supports and confirms what is out there. There is mutuality in his pictures — although often enough of a violent and aggressive kind — but there is never reserve, never objectivity, never analysis. The contrast between his technical virtuosity and the quality of his vision is an interesting one. Many artists since Gauguin have assumed a primitivistic technique in the pursuit of a hyper-sophisticated idea. But Soutine's case is the reverse of this: his vision is primitive, not primitivistic. It reminds us of the Fuegian's seven-syllabled pre-grammatical word. It reminds us of the language of children who naturally make associations between appearances and emotional characteristics:

'It was reported that children, asked to group sets of meaningless drawings, called one set "prickly" and another set "mean" . . . These emotional characteristics seem in some cases to look to the child more striking than do the shape characteristics which appear more obvious to us. At the same time, the importance of this feature of the children's perceptions should not be exaggerated. It seems possible that children are normally most concerned to find out how things work and what they can do with them. It is only in situations where this is impossible that they tend to liken their activities to those of human beings. This may occur with the heavenly bodies, the sun, moon or stars which the child can neither understand nor experiment with. And it may also occur when the child is set what appears to him rather a meaningless task, such as grouping shapes.' (M. D. Vernon, *The Psychology of Perception*, London 1962.)

Although Soutine painting an ox's carcass in his reeking studio in the Rue du Mont St Gothard may seem a far cry from a group of normal children being set 'meaningless' tasks by perceptual psychologists, this account does have a speculative bearing on him. Soutine does identify the emotional characteristics of things; he is not interested in how things work and what he can do with them — and this is exactly what distinguishes him from the French tradition. It is exactly the difference between his Chartres and Corot's, or between his personifications and Picasso's. Is it possible that in a certain way the very activity of painting was a 'meaningless task' — he came to it, after all, out of the blue — one which could only be given 'meaning' by an emotional endowment from outside? Certainly Soutine's apparent indifference to the formal thinking of his contemporaries would appear to confirm this. It meant nothing to him: 'In 1938 he told René Gimpel that Cubism was cerebral, incapable of giving joy, that Cézanne — in whom he had once believed — was too stiff, too recondite, too difficult, too mental.'

One might carry this point further by asking whether the exile which had removed him so finally from his earliest surroundings had not placed him at a remove from the workings and the uses of things, a remove which could again only be bridged by an ecstatic emotional identification with things. The American painter Jack Tworkov, himself an emigré, has commented that Soutine never had an opportunity to exorcise his childhood; he contrasts his deprivation with Cézanne's commanding return to Provence.

And indeed there is a terrible poignancy in Soutine's closeness to the things he paints, his identification with them. He seems to cling to them, to bury himself in them. Everything that he paints is like a close-up, not only because he eliminates the space that separates him from the object but because of the extreme plasticity of the image that he makes of it. Look at the *Page Boy at Maxim's* (plate 32). The boy cut off just below the hips, elbows out, crams the canvas. He jerks forward, jostles us. He can be closer yet, his arms are like jug-handles, the gaps that they make would take our fingers, we could pick him up. He can come closer yet: features are like momentary grimaces. There is an invitation to mimic the pursing of his lips. The head is not like any head we have seen, but it is terribly like a head that we know: our own. We know other people's heads by their symmetry; symmetry is an external quality that separates itself from whatever is not symmetrical. We know our own head by the action of its parts: an eye rubbed, a lip bitten, a corner of the brow cutting into the supporting hand. None of this adds up to 'likeness', nor to a discrete form with proportions, a characteristic symmetry. But it is us, the theatre of our awareness.

The pageboy's face is both profile and head on, his left eye and brow agree with the hook of his nose, his right eye agrees with his brow. Far from fragmenting the head, this twist suggests a more inclusive whole, within which we seem ourselves to be mysteriously included. But he can come even closer: we cannot conceptualise the figure, or detach it from the terms in which it is presented to us. Look at the arm on our right. Is the arm a form which stands over against the background or is it created by the background? Is it an arm which has led to paint being put in a certain place or is it something that has happened out of the paint? The ground nibbles at the arm, cutting into it, destroying its expected arm-ness. Neither arm nor ground takes precedence. What dominates is the paint which we feel as something active, both as matter and as gesture, as colour and as paste. There is no point at which we can unravel the process which led from pageboy to the artist's hand and eye to the canvas. All distances have been eliminated.

Writing about Soutine in 1950, Jack Tworkov suggested that one of the reasons why Soutine had been only lately fully appreciated by American artists was that he looked too reactionary; another was that technically he 'defies analysis of how to do it. But it is precisely this impenetrability to logical analysis as far as his method is concerned, that quality of the surface which appears as if it had "happened" rather than as "made" which unexpectedly reminds us of the most original section of the new painting in this country.' And it is still true. More than any other painter of his generation he evokes abstract expressionism, not exactly through his forms or his picture structures — although de Kooning and others are said to have looked at him closely, and American critics have been at pains to relate his work to New York painting — but through the ethic of his approach. The content of his painting is located similarly, not in a view of the world, nor in a criterion, still less a recipe, for a finished picture. It is first and last in the painting of the picture. Every picture is like a discovery of painting, in the course of which the paint (mere coloured material) becomes one with the subject. Unless the double sensation — of feathers, say, and paint, of looking and painting — is fused, no picture resulted, nothing came. For there was no alternative to fall back on: no theory of how the picture should work, no programme. Only the creative act.

He could not distance himself from the painting experience so that he could see the picture as a free-standing object. This is made apparent by his repeated failure of pictorial scale — which is simply the artist's own perspective on his work. As David Sylvester has put it, he could not see 'that there is a right physical size for every image'. Clement Greenberg, approaching the same point from a different angle, has said that he was not able to bring the illustrative demands of the picture into line with its formal demands. Two examples make the point: the *Carcass of Beef* (plate 28), where he crudely equates the subject and the picture, as though trying to stun himself with the carcass-like dimensions of the canvas; and the *Chartres Cathedral* (plate 40) where the figure in the foreground introduces a scale which is totally denied by the painting of the spires, a perspective which, when the picture is viewed as a whole, vitiates the physical mass of the spires.

He knew nothing of that critical feed-back which is the basis of the most stable forms of art. This is not to say that he was not critical of his work, once he had done it. The reverse is true. But while painting, he was controlled by sensation. Sensation was what he painted about and what he was painting with. It was the fusion of the two that agitated him. Stable art, classic art, by contrast, involves a controlled, deliberate splitting of the painter's relationship with the subject. It insists that his attention to it should oscillate between feeling it as part of himself, part of his continuous experience of the world, and as something outside himself, a discrete object with a life of its own in which he has no part. Equally, his relation to the picture oscillates between distance and closeness, between knowing it as an object and as a deed, or as an intention and as sensation, or as past and future and as also present. This is what Matisse was talking about when he said simply that the tomato he painted was not the same tomato as the one he ate. Against this remark we might oppose the account of Soutine deliberately fasting in front of the steak that he was painting. For him the picture became the very steak that he hungered for. Painting the steak, he also gobbled it.

Success or failure was not therefore a matter of whether the picture was a 'good picture', but rather whether in painting it the identification held true. It was not a matter of finding an enduring solution to an external problem, but of an experience adequately sustained. That this was the mood he worked in is borne out by the accounts of his later life, when work became difficult for him. Wheeler makes the suggestion that 'the secret of his particular expressionism may have been only *how* to express not what', and that as his fluency increased so the spur to paint decreased. It is a convincing comment, in no way weakened by the evidence of those late pictures which were clearly difficult for him to do. Waldemar George, who knew him all his adult life, writes that 'Strange as it seemed, Soutine dreamed of art as a craft. Above all, he was concerned with the professional aspect. He never spoke of a work's soul nor of its lyric content, nor of the intention behind it.'

The very fabric of his painting affects us as an active experience. His works defy words — that is their point. More specifically they defy discussion. We cannot say confidently that they are about anything, nor can we say that they *intend* anything. Still less can we apply the kind of formal analysis that works when a painter's method is near the surface. Do concepts exist in Soutine? Again and again we are left with sensations and paint and sensations-in-paint. He is like a man painting out of darkness, filling his dark world with things and people. Nothing is interchangeable, nothing is carried over from one thing to the next: he can paint a dozen turkeys and each picture is like the first discovery of a turkey. Each turkey had to be lived, to be made part of himself, and the painting of it had also to be lived on the same plane, to be brought wholly into the present. The paint-matter had to be made part of him and part of his living of the turkey. His handling of it must be naive, bringing nothing from the past of skill or knowledge or practice; it had also to be virtuoso, allowing no reconsiderations and no backward glances.

His best pictures are unquestionable, like the things they are of. The *Hanging Turkey* (plate 29) is more a turkey than a version of a turkey. Its surface yields a primitive experience, which we can only extend beyond the name 'Turkey' by a kind of verbal subterfuge. A wing is an unimaginable run of paint, black, forked, flicked, shot with red. The concept 'wing' is left standing by the paint which seems instantly and out of nowhere to generate silky feathers and limp dead-turkey joints. To follow the shape of the carcass against the wall is to have to discover it every inch of the way. There is no tune to pick up, no past or future. You have to listen for each note as it comes. Look at the shape of the blue wall as it is marked out by the bird. Neither shape exists without the other, but theirs is not an aesthetic relationship, a balance in space. The relation between them is one of violent mutuality. In such passages as these you have the feeling that Soutine is inventing painting while you look.

OUTLINE BIOGRAPHY OF SOUTINE

1893	Chaim Soutine born in Smilovitchi, near Minsk, Lithuanian Russia. (1894 was accepted as his birth date until discovery by M. Pierre Courthion of the correct date.) Soutine was the tenth of the eleven children of a Jewish tailor. His childhood was povertystricken. Left home with a friend, Michel Kikoine, who also wanted to be a painter. Studied under a teacher called Krueger in Minsk. Supported himself working as a photographic retoucher.
1910	Vilna. Soutine failed the entrance examination to the School of Fine. Art, but was admitted after he had received private tuition from one of the staff. Worked at the school for three years, partly supported by a doctor.
1913	Paris, where Kikoine and another fellow-student from Vilna, Pinchus Kremegne, had preceded him. Enrolled in class of Cormon at the École des Beaux Arts, but did not stay long. Studio in block in Rue Dantzig known as *La Ruche* (the Beehive). Among his neighbours were Chagall, Kisling, Léger. Soutine also knew Laurens, Pascin, Lipchitz, Miestchaninoff, Coubine, Zadkine, and Modigliani with whom he became friendly. Extreme poverty.
1916	Studio in Cité Falguière where many of his neighbours were sculptors. Introduced by Modigliani to the poet-dealer Zborowski, who began to take an interest in his work.
1918	Brief visit to Cagnes, on the Mediterranean coast.
1919	With Zborowski's help Soutine travels to Céret in the Pyrenees, where Picasso, Gris, Kisling and others had worked before the war.
1920—22	Soutine divides his time between Céret, Paris and Cagnes, spending most of his time at Céret. He returned to Paris in the winter of 1922 with two hundred paintings.
1923	Large number of his pictures are bought by the American collector Dr. Albert C. Barnes, who was in Paris looking for new talent. This event made Soutine's reputation, and from now on he enjoyed financial security. Paul Guillaume publishes first article on Soutine.
1924	Soutine works at Cagnes and Paris. Barnes publishes article on Soutine.
1925	Paris. Studio in the Rue du Mont-St-Gothard, where he installed the carcass of an ox.

34

1926	Paris. Rue de l'Aude. Still-lifes of dead fowl. First pictures of liveried hotel employees.
1927	Paris. Visits Blanc, Indre.
1928	Paris. Avenue du Parc Montsouris. Monograph on Soutine by Waldemar George.
1929	Paris. Chatel Guyon. Monograph on Soutine by Élie Faure.
1930	Passage d'Enfer. Illness.
1931—5	Paris. Summers at Château de Lèves, near Chartres, the property of Marcellin and Madeleine Castaing, who during the last few years had become his most important collectors.
1935	First major exhibition, at the Arts Club of Chicago.
1936—7	Paris. Avenue d'Orléans.
1938—9	Paris. Villa Seurat.
1940	Soutine leaves Paris and settles temporarily at Civry. Refuses invitation to go to America, in spite of his perilous position under the German occupation.
1941—3	At Champigny-sur-Veuldre, Indre. Now severely attacked by the stomach ulcers he had suffered from for much of his life. He collapses in the summer of 1943 and is driven in a desperate condition to Paris, where he dies after an operation on August 9th. Buried at the cemetery of Montparnasse, Picasso and Cocteau being among the few who follow the coffin.

NOTE ON SOUTINE'S TECHNIQUE

Soutine invariably painted from nature, not from drawings or memory, and his canvases were therefore not usually very large, particularly those worked out of doors. His largest pictures were those done from the carcass of an ox about 1925. He usually painted on canvas, but there is a number of works of the early 'thirties painted on wooden panels. He also liked to paint on old pictures he bought up at junk markets. This may explain the dubious condition of many of his pictures.

No drawings as such are known to the author. It has been stated that Soutine at one time destroyed a quantity of drawings, but Mlle 'Garde' (the companion of the last years of his life) contradicts this, saying that she never saw Soutine draw, not even 'machinalement sur les nappes en papier comme tous les peintres. Il commençait directement sur la toile avec la couleur, sans dessin préalable.' However, Leymarie has recently published three heads drawn in charcoal on canvas which could well be the preparatory stages of paintings that were never continued.

Mlle 'Garde' states that Soutine hesitated for a long time in front of the subject before starting to paint (see note to plate 46). Once he had started, he worked with abandon. He did not, like an Impressionist, limit his working to a particular condition of light. Many pictures appear to have been completed extremely rapidly: Wheeler states that 'his usual practice was to complete each picture in a single working session'. If the picture did not satisfy him next day, he started again on a new canvas.

One of the most surprising impressions that one receives from Soutine's work in the flesh, is of the great clarity and delicacy of the paint. It has none of the crudities that are common in expressionist art, or the tortured quality that one might expect from the quality of the image. Wheeler states that he habitually used a different brush 'one for each nuance of colour and for each magnitude of brush-stroke, beginning with about forty of them and discarding them on the ground as fast as he used them'.

Soutine was a prolific painter, working in bursts of furious activity. He also destroyed a great deal. Indeed it has been reckoned that only one out of ten of his canvases survive. Apart from the quantities that he destroyed as he worked on them, he tried to eradicate his earlier production completely. He came to detest his works of the Céret period and in later years he bought them back whenever he could, expressly to destroy them. This explains why by far the largest part of the early work is now in America.

36

NOTES ON THE PLATES

Most of the pictures reproduced here were photographed when they were in London on the occasion of the Arts Council exhibition at the Tate Gallery in 1963. Inevitably the following notes lean heavily on the catalogue to that exhibition. In his introductory note to the Tate catalogue entries Mr Maurice Tuchman (who is preparing a *catalogue raisonné* of Soutine's oeuvre) comments on the confusion that has surrounded many aspects of Soutine's work:

'Even Élie Faure's little monograph ... written rather early in Soutine's career by a brilliant art historian who knew the artist personally, contains surprising misdates of then recent paintings ... The fact that many scores of important Soutines, concentrated in a few private collections, have never been exhibited or photographed, has also obscured our view of the painter and has facilitated the acceptance of false works begun by Soutine, discarded, and completed by other hands.'

Plate 1 *Still-life with Lemons.* c. 1916. 25¾ × 21¼ in. (65.5 × 54 cm.). Mr and Mrs Irving Levick, Buffalo, N.Y.

Several of these still-lifes exist among Soutine's earliest works, in which a few objects are arranged on a table top. The most characteristic feature of his vision has already declared itself — the lively, almost anthropomorphic drawing of the fork seems to endow it with an energetic and slightly sinister personality of its own.

Plate 2 *Portrait of the Painter Richard.* c. 1916—17. 21¾ × 17¾ in. (55 × 45 cm.). McRoberts and Tunnard Ltd., London.

His sitters at this time were often fellow artists from the crowded studios of *La Ruche.* He himself sat on two occasions for Modigliani.

This picture gives us some insight into the foundations of Soutine's style. It is a tightly drawn and densely modelled work which indicates his profound debt to Cézanne.

Plate 3 *Jug with Lilacs.* c. 1917—18. 21⅝ × 18¼ in. (55 × 46.5 cm.). Mr & Mrs Matthew H. Futter, New York.

Soutine made a large number of flower paintings during the years in Paris before he went to Céret (a fine example is illustrated in Wheeler, p. 37). David Sylvester draws attention to Soutine's debt to Bonnard in these pictures, which is to be seen particularly in the surface quality of the brush-strokes.

Plate 4 *Still-life with Fish.* c. 1918. 16¼ × 25¼ in. (41 × 64 cm.). Miss Adelaide Milton de Groot, New York.

This, like the *Still-life with Lemons* (plate 1), is like a crude but vigorous anticipation of aspects of the later still-lifes. The wriggling curves of the fish, their staring eyes and gaping mouths, have a tremendous force. But the distortions of the subject have not found the freedom in movement that they will soon have, partly because he has not yet achieved a strong relationship between the main forms and their field.

Plate 5 *Self-portrait.* c. 1918. 21½ × 18 in. (54.5 × 46 cm.). Collection of Mr and Mrs Henry Pearlman, New York.

'Perhaps Soutine's first authentic image', in Maurice Tuchman's words. It is interesting to note the difference of psychological viewpoint between this painting and the *Portrait of Richard* (plate 2). The earlier picture seems to be seen at a distance — the self-portrait in close-up. The difference of feeling is embodied in the careful modelling of the one and in the agitated handling and the stressed drawing of the other.

Plate 6 *Trees at Céret.* c. 1919. 21¼ × 28¾ in. (54 × 73 cm.). The Ben Uri Art Gallery, London.

This picture is among the earliest Céret landscapes and indicates how completely Soutine threw himself into the pursuit of a total pictorial movement. The nature of the subject helps. Just as the fishes in the still-life (plate 4) led him to a special movement, so here the dark, writhing tree trunks bring a single violent convulsion to the picture surface.

Plate 7 *Peasant Boy.* c. 1919—20. 24½ × 21 in. (62 × 53.5 cm.). Mr and Mrs Ralph F. Colin, New York.

Tuchman draws attention to something in this picture which was to be a recurrent feature of Soutine's portraits: 'the ambiguous marking of the subject's right shoulder; we cannot be sure exactly where the shoulder ends'. It is a familiar characteristic of artists who work from the model that they seem to discover especially loaded problems or special ambiguities in certain forms, which they return to over and over again as if everything depended on them. Shoulders seem to have held such obsessive mysteries for Soutine; he stresses them, distorts them, gives them a peculiar emphasis or seems to call an unsuspected life out of them while, at the same time, as Tuchman says, clearly finding a particular difficulty in drawing them.

Plate 8 *Man Praying.* c. 1920. 36 × 21 in. (91 × 54 cm.). The Perls Galleries, New York.

There are several of these extraordinary pictures from the Céret period in which the sitter is inordinately elongated, and an agitated, drawn out flicker seems to run down the length of the figure. It is not a distortion of the kind that we know in the later portraits where we locate the oddities of drawing in the features of the sitter. The figure is remarkably intact in spite of his elongation. We attribute the distortion to the painter, not to the model. It has been said that he is here looking at his sitter as though at a landscape. Sylvester has drawn attention to the resemblance between this picture and Giacometti's bronze heads, *Têtes tranchantes.*

Plate 9 *Gorge du Loup.* c. 1920—21. 32 × 31 in. (81 × 79 cm.). The Henry Pearlman Foundation, New York.

One of the features that Soutine developed in the Céret landscapes was a low vantage point which placed the horizon at the very top of the picture. This is one of the first pictures constructed like this. The point of this feature is that it brings all parts of the canvas into a similar relation to the landscape. It alleviates a particular difficulty which, as painters concerned themselves more and more with the flat character of the canvas, had become one of the key problems of landscape painting: the split between land and sky. To paint from a low vantage point was the landscape equivalent to the device of tilting the table top in a still-life (as Cézanne had done) rather than looking across it (as Chardin had done). Soutine would have been forced to think about landscape in this way simply because he was painting in a mountainous district; but these exigencies would have appeared doubly

meaningful to him because of his developing interest in a shallow pictorial space.

Plate 10 *Landscape at Céret.* c. 1920—21. 24 × 32 in. (61 × 81.5 cm.). E. & A. Silberman Galleries, New York.

Soutine's handling of paint is becoming more fluid and less linear as the movement in his pictures becomes more closely related to a shallow space.

Plate 11 *Landscape, Céret.* c. 1920—21. 21¼ × 36¼ in. (54 × 92 cm.). Fogg Art Museum, Harvard University (gift of Mr & Mrs Ralph F. Colin).

Plate 12 *Landscape at Céret.* c. 1920—21. 24 × 33 in. (61 × 84 cm.). Tate Gallery, London.

One of the finest of the Céret landscapes. This picture embodies the mysteries of the whole series. It 'has nothing to do with the experience of *gazing* at a landscape. Here is a jungle of colour, layer upon impenetrable layer, not murky but of a luxurious darkness in which light is held as in porphyry or jasper or chalcedony. It is a light that belongs to the forms, not a light thrown upon them. The atmosphere, similarly, has nothing to do with how the weather is behaving in a given area at a certain time (and to give these landscapes, as some do, such titles as *Mistral* or *Storm at Céret* is like believing that *Pilgrim's Progress* is the story of a hiking tour). Whether it is noon or dusk, whether it is raining or the wind is blowing, is of no concern. Nor is it really a matter of importance what things the shapes stand for — that this is a hill or a house or a tree. We acknowledge that it is, but we get no feeling — such as we do before a Matisse, a Bonnard, a Picasso — that this particular transformation of an object is making us *see* this kind of object in a new way. We do not read this landscape in terms of objects and relations between objects. Our awareness cuts through objects. It responds to rhythms, to an interplay of forces. To the opposition, for example, on the left-hand side of the picture, between the hectic downward-rushing movement of the torpedo shape (the foliage of a tree) and the slow, straining, upward-mounting movement of the two pyramids (the house and the hill) one of which rises out of and above the other. As it reaches the upper apex, goes over the top, this striving motion suddenly explodes into a paroxysm of movement and counter-movement, into abandon and release. And the other experiences the painting evokes are of a kind that engage our whole bodies: swinging, diving, falling, staggering, skating climbing, gliding, riding downhill, teetering on a cliff edge. It evokes them as if they were dissociated from any firm contact with external objects. We enact them as we act in a nightmare, in the void of a nightmare. They arouse panic: only this panic is resolved, for the opposing forces are all somehow contained and held in balance by the overriding rhythm of the picture as a whole — not a frantic but an easy rhythm, like the swinging of a pendulum — which resolves convulsion and conflict into an unexpected serenity.' (David Sylvester, in his introduction to the Arts Council exhibition catalogue, 1963.)

Plate 13 *Hill at Céret.* c. 1921. 29 × 21¾ in. (73.5 × 55 cm.). Perls Galleries, New York.

This represents the most extreme development of Soutine's Céret style. The landscape is drowned deep in his subjectivity. Indeed, the kinds of movement that he has evolved and the close all-over grey-green tones make it impossible to see the landscape at a distance. Where so little is specific in descriptive terms and so much in pictorial terms, fantasy takes over. It is about this picture that Thomas B. Hess's famous lines are written:

'I see the hill with a house on top, but below, and to the left, I find a hook-nosed witch, a handkerchief tied around her head, holding the collar of a squatting dragon. But the beast's right side is defined by a dark area which now appears to be a curling-horned steer, drastically foreshortened, rising up to the farmhouse, while below, guarding his eyes with his forearm, a man tumbles backward into the sea. A few minutes later, I might have difficulty in finding some of these forms again. Perhaps the landscape will return, with all its roads, banks of trees, coils of earth, and flying clouds. But the very manipulation of pigment has pried the subject from nature into the personal sensation of terror, violence — and paint. Such a picture repays hours of examination, for it is fitted together as deftly as any Cubist portrait. Interweaving layers of hue, coiled lines that shoot and cage motion within the rectangle, the elaborate play of tonalities up and down the image, all suggest spontaneity, but also disclose the patience and the labour involved. That the landscape is filled with animal energy, at times sinister, at times benevolently pastoral, is a logical projection of Soutine's vision. Everything in the painting breathes and devours space and colour. Nature is again populated with demi-gods who re-sanctify their ancient myths under the most banal fields or within everyday trees.' (Thomas B. Hess, *Abstract Painting: Background and American Phase*, New York, 1951.)

Plate 14 *Village Square, Céret.* c. 1921—2. 29⅞ × 33¾ in. (76 × 85.5 cm.). The Henry Pearlman Foundation, New York.

This picture reminds us of Soutine's relationship to Cubism. Because he is dealing with buildings, he is deal-ing with angular movements and flat surfaces and this inevitably modifies the composition. The picture surface itself becomes flat and angular and the shallow quasi-cubist space is more closely controlled. As so often in these pictures, this one is difficult to read in a literal way, even though whole houses and hints of other houses and trees and hills are plain to see. But it is a marvellously satisfying composition, as energetic as any, but more contained, more finely balanced than earlier pictures.

Plate 15 *Red Roofs, Céret.* c. 1921—2. 32 × 25⅜ in. (81 × 64.5 cm.). The Henry Pearlman Foundation, New York.

As if searching for something to check himself against, Soutine began to introduce buildings as the main features of the later Céret pictures. Movements in these pictures seem to have nothing of the lopsided, unbraced, vertiginous quality that we see in the earlier works, but to have instead a complex and precarious balance. In the *Village Square* (plate 14), a centralised pyramid anchors the whole picture. Here the buildings establish a kind of grid which is fixed at the edges of the canvas by the two trees, almost as if they were window frames. This concern for a more stable framework can be seen as a tentative retreat from the extreme subjectivity of the *Hill at Céret* of 1919—20.

Plate 16 *Hill at Céret.* c. 1922. 28½ × 35¾ in. (72.5 × 91 cm.). Perls Galleries, New York.

A complete change of attitude is heralded here. Tuchman suggests that in view of its much lighter tonality it was probably painted after Soutine had visited Cagnes on the Mediterranean coast. It represents the hill at Céret, but the way in which the subject is seen is in total contrast with the earlier picture. Now the hill is set back into the canvas as if into a niche. It makes a clear shape that we can grasp as a whole; so do the individual cypresses and bushes and houses on the hill. This is a quite different expression of space — we can enter the picture at the bottom and proceed upwards. All this betokens a greater psychological distance from the subject. He is no longer so totally immersed in it, but is to some extent standing back from his experience of it and trying to regulate his account of it. His efforts to do this result in something which seems naive by comparison with the earlier pictures, although the effort itself was the reverse.

Plate 17 *Landscape with Cypresses.* c. 1922—3. 26 × 32 in. (66 × 87 cm.). Mr and Mrs Albert A. List, New York.

This is one of the most interesting points of transition between the styles of Céret and Cagnes. The central part of the subject is fragmented, agitated: we feel that he has lost himself in it in a mood that recalls the Céret vision but the *mise en scène* is quite different. The central passage is situated at a distance by the road that wanders along the bottom of the picture and up into the left corner; and the sky too, making a clean horizon line, introduces a further progression which includes the overlapping, scaled buildings on the right.

Plate 18 *Landscape with Road, Cagnes.* c. 1923. 25 × 30 in. (63.5 × 76 cm.). Rex de C. Nan Kivell, Esq., London.

As Soutine pushes the subject further back and transfers the pictorial movements from the brush mark to the landscape features themselves — as if reflecting on his own fantasy instead of painting in the grip of it — a note of elegance enters his work for the first time. The appearance of figures in these pictures is significant too, denoting a further stage in his withdrawal. He is dramatising the situation as well as experiencing it.

Plate 19 *Landscape at Cagnes.* c. 1923. 21¼ × 25½ in. (54 × 64.5 cm.). Pierre Lévy, Troyes.

Plate 20 *Side of Beef.* c. 1923. 27½ × 20½ in. (70 × 52 cm.). Mr and Mrs Ralph F. Colin, New York.

This appears to be the first of Soutine's studies of raw meat.

'In the late 'twenties', Wheeler tells us, 'one scarcely heard mention of Soutine without some scandalised discourse about the gruesome circumstances of their production. When he lived in *La Ruche*, he had made friends with slaughterhouse employees and practised painting pieces of meat which he got from them. (None of these is now known.) About 1922 he painted an admirable *Side of Beef* in forthright realism, with the vivid red of steak, the ivory and pale gold of suet, and a finely realised hollowness inside the curved ribs.'

Plate 21 *Woman in Red.* c. 1923. 25 × 21 in. (65.5 × 53.5 cm.). Dr and Mrs Harry Bakwin, New York.

Perhaps the most extraordinary of all Soutine's portraits, this picture combines in a uniquely pointed way his pictorial daring and his feeling for the actuality of the subject. It is interesting that at some time or other the fantastic sweeping curves of the hat were felt to be too extreme: the hat was repainted and its character considerably reduced by another hand, as one can see

from the reproduction of the picture in Wheeler which was made before the picture was cleaned.

Plate 22 *Still-life with Fish, Eggs and Lemons.* c. 1923. 25½ × 31⅝ in. (65 × 80.5 cm.). Marlborough Fine Art Ltd., London.

The work of the mid and late 'twenties often shows a certain naive grandiosity, as in the *Woman in Red* (plate 21) or in the curve of the table here and the gigantic scale of the bread. We feel it, too, in the curious, almost heraldic arrangement, which was present in the earlier still-lifes, but is now far more conscious, regular and elaborate: the four fish matched by pairs of eggs and lemons, the bread bisected exactly by the flask. The arrangements of other still-lifes of the time are almost as contrived as the set-pieces that one sees on high-class fishmonger's slabs.

Plate 23 *Still-life with Red Meat.* c. 1923—4. 21¼ × 25⅝ in. (54 × 65 cm.). M. Pierre Lévy, Troyes.

A remarkable picture in which Soutine seems to be experimenting with new viewpoints. The asymetrical disposition of the picture makes a strange contrast with the regular arrangement of the objects that one can just see at the top of the table. Also uncharacteristic of Soutine is the freely painted, almost decorative, notation with which he describes the turned legs of the table.

David Sylvester has connected this work with Bonnard. Certainly no one understood the possibilities of this kind of off-centre composition as well as Bonnard.

Plate 24 *Beef and Calf's Head.* c. 1924. 36¼ × 28¾ in. (92 × 73 cm.). Mme Jean Walter, Paris.

In contrast with the earlier pictures, this carcass is not modelled in depth. Here Soutine is exploring the most direct relationship between the paint and the subject, working as though the paint itself had become meat in his mind, as though the yellow paint *was* fat, rather than the means to describe fat, and the red *was* lean.

Plate 25 *Houses at Cagnes.* c. 1924. 21⅝ × 18⅛ in. (55 × 46.5 cm.). George Waechter Memorial Foundation, Geneva.

Soutine continued to work at Cagnes for spells during the summer for several years, the last being in 1925.

Plate 26 *Hare on a Green Shutter.* c. 1924—5. 31⅞ × 21¼ in. (81 × 54 cm.). M. Pierre Lévy, Troyes.

Soutine made about twelve pictures of dead hares or rabbits hanging by their feet. The powerful silhouette of the animal yields an expressive image of the utmost power, which becomes more and more rich as Soutine repeats it and explores its nuances. In several works the form of the hind legs is repeated with powerful effect in the folds of the drapery against which it is hanging, as though he is singling out the dominant form and amplifying it as pure expression. This picture is rather untypical of the series, with its specific background of a shutter. Usually the ground is less particular.

Plate 27 *Fish and Tomatoes*. c. 1925. 25¼ × 33½ in. (64 × 85 cm.). Jack and Lillian Poses, New York.

Soutine returns to the still-life theme of a centralised plate and symmetrically placed forks, after having left it for several years. The heraldic regularity of arrangement, noticed earlier, is very much in evidence. So too is the anthropomorphism which is so characteristic of his vision. There is a suggestion of bloody, self-destructive violence in the image: one can see it as a head crowned with red, grasping hands raised. Sylvester goes further: 'the forks resting on either side of the plate of fish immediately suggest someone's hands ripping his stomach apart and laying bare his entrails — an image reinforced by the red of the tomatoes against the white of the napkin'.

Plate 28 *Carcass of Beef*. c. 1925. 55¼ × 42⅜ in. (140 × 107.5 cm.). The Albright-Knox Art Gallery, Buffalo, N.Y.

Inspired by Rembrandt's *Slaughtered Ox* in the Louvre, it was typical that Soutine should reconstruct the subject from nature. Everything suggests that he saw the beef pictures as masterworks: the giant scale, the almost incredible fanaticism with which he worked at them.

Wheeler tells us that 'in 1925, when he had a studio large enough in the Rue du Mont-St-Gothard, he procured the entire carcass of a steer, and it was this undertaking which grew legendary. He did at least four (large) canvases, ... as well as sketches and smaller canvases; and meantime the steer decomposed. According to the legend, when the glorious colours of the flesh were hidden ... by an accumulation of flies, he paid a wretched little model to sit beside it and fan them away. He got from the butcher a pail of blood, so that when a portion of the beef dried out, he could freshen its colour. Other dwellers in the Rue du Mont-St-Gothard complained of the odour of rotting flesh, and when the police arrived Soutine harangued them on how much more important art was than sanitation.'

Plate 29 *Hanging Turkey*. c. 1926. 36 × 28½ in. (91.5 × 72.5 cm.). Mr. Richard S. Zeisler, New York.
Even more important than the hare and rabbits, and,

it could be argued, more successful than the beefs, is a series of pictures of hanging fowl. There are more than twenty of them, turkeys, ducks, chickens, some plucked, some in full feather, some hanging alone as here, others grouped with tomatoes.

They represent the highest point of his achievement in still-life. The dead bird becomes, like the trees in his last landscapes, an eloquent and flexible vehicle into which he concentrates a vast range of feeling. Tuchman comments: 'The series may be divided into two types: a restless, baroque deployment of open, agitated shapes and swirling lines filling most of the canvas — found in pictures where the fowl is upside down; and a quieter, more self-contained and vertical placement with subtle, nervous movements (rather than dramatic thrusts of shape) — found in pictures where the fowl hangs by the neck'.

Soutine explores the expressive possibilities of the plumage, spread wide or folded sleekly, almost as though it were an abstract language, fulfilling a role analogous to drapery in earlier art.

Plate 30 *Fowl*. c. 1926. 37¾ × 28⅜ in. (96 × 72 cm.). M. Pierre Wertheimer, Paris.

These are Soutine's most individualised images. Even more than in his portraits one feels his avid attention to the particulars of the subject, the way in which he seizes on and questions the character of every feature as though it constituted a gesture in its own right.

It is noticeable that the relation of the main form to the background is far more dense and substantial here than in most of his other pictures. The shapes into which the blue ground is divided make a powerful frame, angular, nervous, but at the same time seeming to have an enormous strength. The surface is realised with an assurance and a command of matière that reminds us of Courbet.

Plate 31 *Still-life with Turkey*. c. 1926. 21¼ × 31⅞ in. (54 × 81 cm.). M. Pierre Lévy, France.

Here the turkey is not alone, but lies like a corpse around which the tomatoes are lined up in a guard of honour and the jug and spoon stand like mourners. Soutine never painted these subjects as previous painters had done, as decorative or formal compositions. Tragedy is never absent, least of all in this composition which is one of the most moving.

Plates 32 and **33** *Page Boy at Maxims*. c. 1927—8. 38¾ × 31½ in. (98 × 80 cm). Musée National d'Art Moderne, Paris. *Page Boy at Maxims.* c. 1926. 32¼ × 29½ in. (82 × 75 cm.). Baronne Alix de Rothschild, Paris.

Soutine became interested in painting uniformed figures at about the same time as he began the still-lifes of dead birds. He was fascinated by the possibilities of colour concentration that the subject opened up, and he explored one colour after another, the white of cooks, the red, dark greens and blues of pageboys and *valets de chambre*, the white and crimson of choir boys. These works were immediately popular and Soutine enjoyed real prosperity on the strength of them.

Plate 34 *Woman Bathing.* c. 1929. 21⅝ × 24⅜ in. (55 × 62 cm.). M. and Mme Marcellin Castaing, Lèves, Eure-et-Loire.

This is another work inspired by Rembrandt (see note on plate 28), in this case the National Gallery's *Woman Bathing*. There are in fact two pictures inspired by this work, both belonging to the Castaing collection. In both, Soutine approaches the figure more frontally than Rembrandt did and brings it into closer range. The second version is nearer to the original than this painting, in which he cuts the figure off at the waist.

As when he was painting the oxcarcass, Soutine went to great lengths to reconstruct the subject from nature. Speaking of the second version, Wheeler records his endless hunt for the right model until one day he found a suitable peasant woman. 'At first she was suspicious of immorality, then fearful of madness, but at last was persuaded to stand in a brook in one corner of the Castaing property . . .' On one occasion while he was painting: 'Clouds suddenly gathered overhead, and it began to rain. The peasant woman cried out to him to stop and let her take shelter somewhere. He shouted orders back at her, not to move an inch or she would be to blame for ruining his work. The rain fell, the thunder rolled, and it was dark, but Soutine went on working . . . At last he came to his senses and was surprised to find himself drenched to the skin, and the model in hysterical tears, shaking with cold and fright.'

Plate 35 *Portrait of Madeleine Castaing.* c. 1928. 39⅜ × 28⅞ in. (100 × 73.5 cm.). Miss Adelaide Milton de Groot, New York.

Mme Castaing and her husband were important figures in Soutine's life from the late 'twenties until his death. They have one of the largest collections of his work. There is a revealing story of their first meeting with Soutine which must have occurred some ten years before they became friendly with him. They had just begun to collect modern art and were on the lookout for young and undiscovered talent. Modigliani advised them to see Soutine who was then quite unknown and in desperate poverty. An appointment was made. Soutine was too shy to meet them in company and they found him on the pavement in front of a café, 'pacing up and down, unprepossessing, overwrought, not at all friendly, with a canvas under his arm. M. Castaing was impressed by his work, there under the streetlight, but wanted to come to the studio where there might be a greater number of pictures to choose from, and offered him an advance of one hundred francs. Soutine would have none of it. "You don't like my painting, you only want to help me. If you had given me one franc for my picture I would have taken it." Then he stalked away by himself and the Castaings saw nothing of him for many years.' (Wheeler.)

Plates 36 and **37** *The Polish Girl.* 1929. 25 × 18⅛ in. (63.5 × 46 cm.). M. Georges Halphen, La Chapelle en Serval, Oise. *Portrait of Lina.* c. 1928–29. 15 × 18¼ in. (38 × 46.5 cm.). Kunstmuseum, Lucerne.

Both this and the last two pictures illustrate a certain change in attitude in Soutine's portraits at this time — there is a more conventional relationship between painter and sitter, a more predictable attention to likeness, a certain suspension of Soutine's own idiosyncrasies. This was at a time when Soutine was coming to terms with an unexpected success. But it would be wrong to look at these pictures for signs of compromise. They are miracles of personalisation.

Plate 38 *Female Nude.* c. 1933. 18¼ × 10⅝ in. (46.5 × 27.5 cm.). Mr and Mrs Ralph F. Colin, New York.

This is the only known nude.

During the early 'thirties a change comes over Soutine's technique, and over the feeling yielded by the paint' which becomes drier, more solid, more slow-moving. His vision seems less obviously tormented and less hectically involved in the life of the object. Many pictures of this time evoke the realism of Courbet, a realism for its own sake rather than for the imaginative expression that can be contained in it.

Plate 39 *Plucked Goose.* c. 1933. 16¼ × 18⅜ in. (41 × 47 cm.). Alex Reid and Lefevre Ltd., London.

This, the only picture of a dead bird done during the 'thirties, illustrates the change of style and feeling. The drama of the earlier still-lifes seems a long way off; it is simply a study of a dead goose, not an image of deadness or of violence in death. His representational virtuosity is at its peak here. The massive painting of the head and body and the way that delicate touches of the brush embellish it with feathers is noteworthy. Wheeler reproduced this picture in his book vertically. It is now agreed, however, that the goose is lying on a table.

Plate 40 *Chartres Cathedral.* c. 1933. 36×19¼ in. (91.5×49.5 cm.). Mrs L. B. Wescott, Rosemont, New Jersey.

Soutine painted this while staying with the Castaings at Lèves near Chartres. He was their guest there during the summers from 1931 to 1935.

Plate 41 *Avenue of Trees.* c. 1936. 30×27¼ in. (76×69 cm.). Mr and Mrs Ralph F. Colin, New York (Property of Pamela T. Colin).

With this picture of the Grand Prés near Chartres, we come to what was to be the last major theme in Soutine's work. In 1929 he had painted a series of pictures of a single tree, the Tree of Vence. Now he turns to avenues and clumps and discovers in their waving branches something of the all-over movement of the Céret landscapes and something of the piercing emotional eloquence of the still-lifes of the 'twenties.

It is noticeable that in these landscapes the calligraphic element of his style reappears.

Plate 42 *Woman Reading.* c. 1936–7. 25½×31¾ in. (65×81 cm.). M. and Mme Marcellin Castaing, Lèves, Eure-et-Loire.

Awkwardness and virtuosity alternate in Soutine's art. This picture looks fumbling, naive, anxious, in contrast to the elegant assurance of, for example, the *Plucked Goose* of only three years earlier. This fact alone speaks of the content of Soutine's art: for him painting was never a foregone conclusion, nor could he tide himself over the difficulties by recourse to theory.

Towards the end of his life Soutine was working very little. Wheeler tells us that he spent a lot of time idling in cafés with sycophantic admirers, lying in hotel bedrooms reading philosophy to improve his mind, sleeping to pass the time. Seen against this background of depression and ennui this picture becomes still more moving.

Plate 43 *Return from School.* c. 1939. 17×18 in. (43×46.5 cm.). Phillips Collection, Washington, D.C.

During the late 'thirties his figure paintings assume a more generalised quality as though he was seeing the figures less as individuals and more as emblems of human situations. The same is true of a number of landscapes in which the composition centres on the figures of children. There is no doubt that in this picture, for

example, he sees the relationship between the violent sky and the sinister trees on the horizon and the little figures hurrying towards us as an image of anxiety and foreboding. Wheeler relates these pictures to a painting by Courbet of two children in a landscape which Soutine had particularly admired some years earlier. Also, when the picture was painted, Soutine was suffering increasingly. As a Jew he had particular reason to dread a war with Germany; to be thinking of refugees.

Plate 44 *Two Children on the Road.* c. 1939. 17¾×25⅛ in. (45×64 cm.). M. Jacques Guérin, Paris.

Both this and the last picture remind us of Soutine's debt to Bonnard, not only with regard to the subject but also in the random-seeming composition and in the way in which the figures are embedded in a lively, flickering coloursurface. But the quality of the image is inimitable: the figures seem to have materialised violently in the landscape; to convey a shock that reminds us of certain effects of the cinema. Wheeler suggests a tribute to Chaplin: Soutine was in fact an addict of the cinema.

Plate 45 *Windy Day, Auxerre.* c. 1939. 19¼×25⅝ in. (49×65 cm.). Phillips Collection, Washington, D.C.

Among the most ambitious of these great last pictures, *Windy Day, Auxerre* has a breadth of implication that is as near as any modern artist has got to the world landscapes of the Old Masters. The relationship between the tiny figures and the soaring trees is profoundly moving: the figures are dominated by the trees, as the trees themselves are dominated and transformed by the roaring wind, the violent, breaking light. Landscape has rarely been painted as so complete an imaginative experience.

The structure of the picture is particularly complex: the brush marks alone are called upon to convey a wide range of meaning, from the solid surfaces of the road, to the almost abstract notation of sky and light, to the free, swirling movements of the trees in the centre, which directly evoke gusts of wind.

Plate 46 *Trees at Auxerre.* c. 1939. 28¾×23¼ in. (73×59.5 cm.). Private Collection, London.

In an account of this period of Soutine's life, Mlle 'Garde', his companion of the time, describes how on his arrival in the country from Paris, Soutine would go out at once searching for trees to paint. 'At last he found a subject. As usual he looked at it a dozen times before deciding to paint it. He went out, came home, returned, made such a coming and going between our house and the motif that he attracted the attention of the police, who, taking him for a particularly dangerous kind of lunatic, did not hesitate to arrest him.' The incident ends with Soutine being vouched for by a friend in high office in Paris, after which he becomes generally respected in the village and referred to as 'the great painter'. 'Garde' also tells how she would persuade children to pose for him on the roads, and had to bribe them with sweets to stand still. When they were stuffed full they would become restless and want to go home.

Plate 47 *The Oak.* c. 1941. $23\frac{5}{8} \times 27\frac{3}{4}$ in. (60×70.5 cm.) M. Pierre Wertheimer, Paris.

Of all the pictures of trees, this one exemplifies most clearly the way in which he uses them as an almost abstract expressive form. The oak fills the canvas. We are immersed in it, a single, simple image in a sense, but with endless ramifications. An outstretched hand, the reefs and inlets of some archipelago of the mind, an explosive out-flying of whirling fragments — these are some of the associations that flood from the original image of the tree.

Plate 48 *Landscape with Reclining Figure.* c. 1942. $28\frac{3}{4} \times 36\frac{1}{4}$ in. (73×92 cm.). Collection of M. Alex Maguy, Galerie de l'Elysée, Paris.

Another version of this picture is reproduced in Wheeler (109). In both the upper right-hand corner is left unpainted, and in both the handling of the rest of the picture has a strange thickness of touch — reminding us again of the alternatives of skill and clumsiness that run through all periods of his work.

Here the figure lies as if watching the trees and their reflections, an observer. The little hut seems to return her stare. In the other version the figure is smaller and her head is buried in her arms. She seems to be prostrated in front of the trees. In both one has the feeling of the human presence and attention interlocked with the landscape, part of it, just as the trees and their reflections interlock and are painted as though part of the same thing. It can be read as an image of his own attitude, an image of mutuality.

I

2

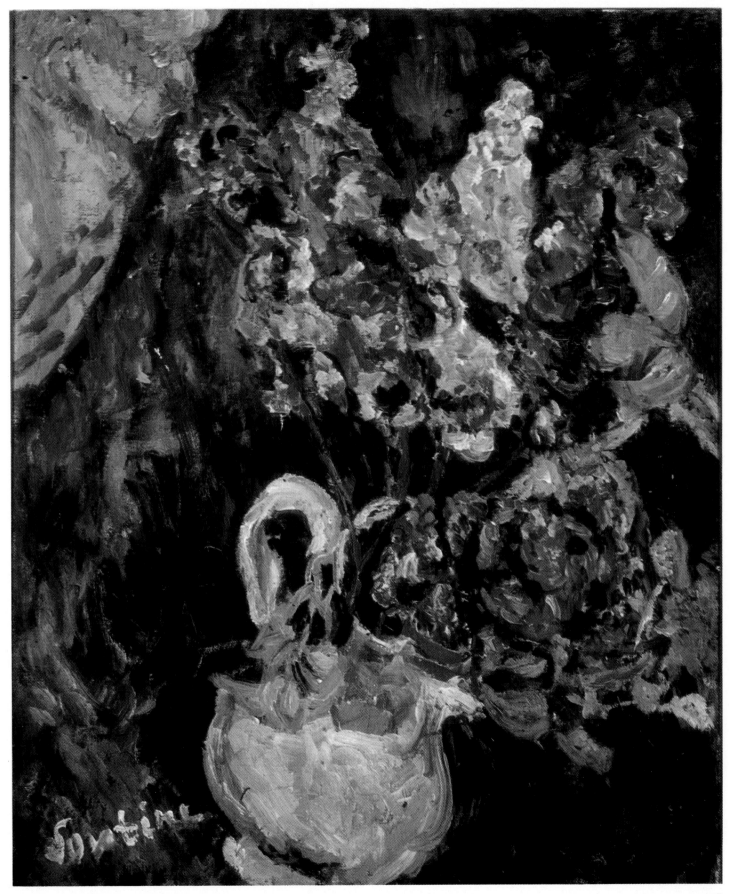

4

6

8

9

10

11

12

14

16

17

18

19

22

23

24

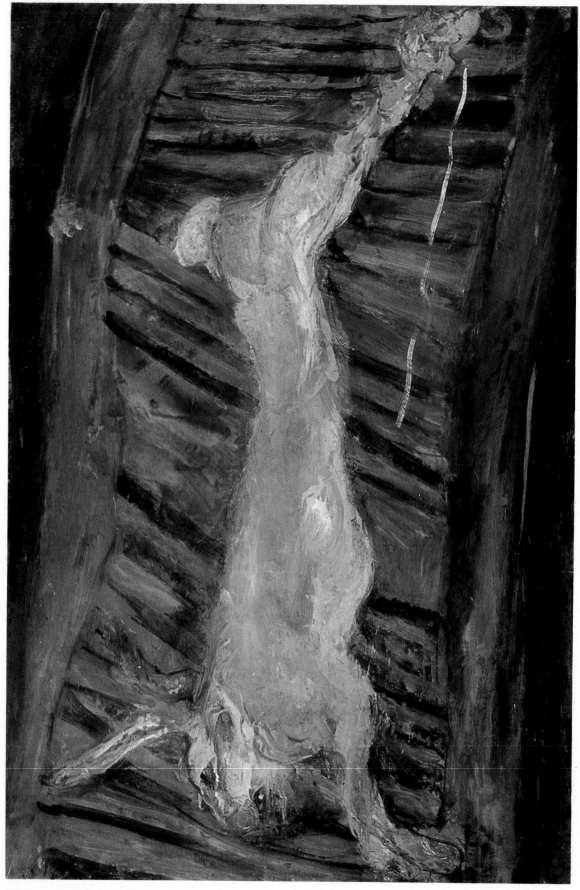

26

27

28

29

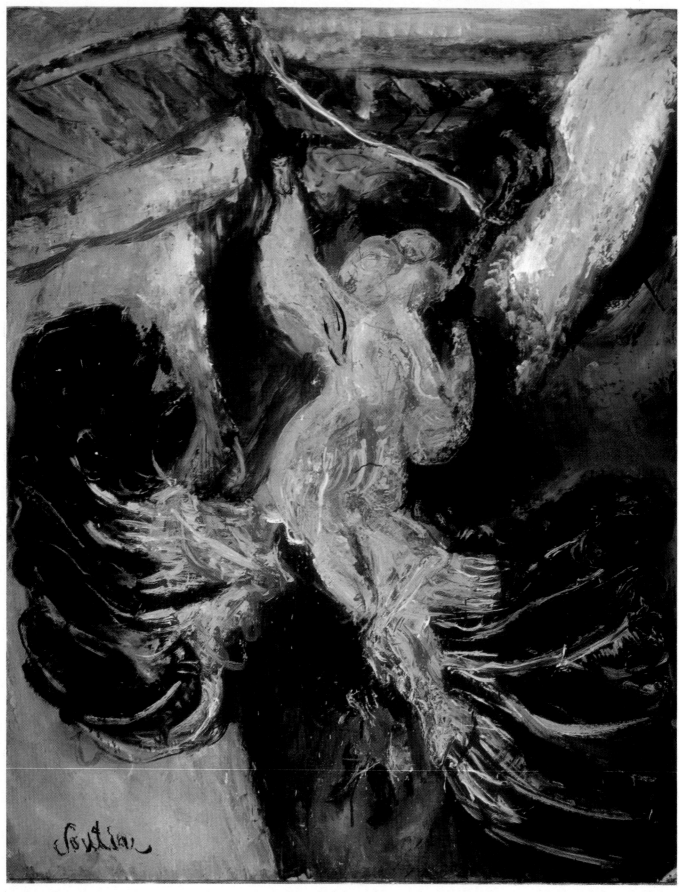

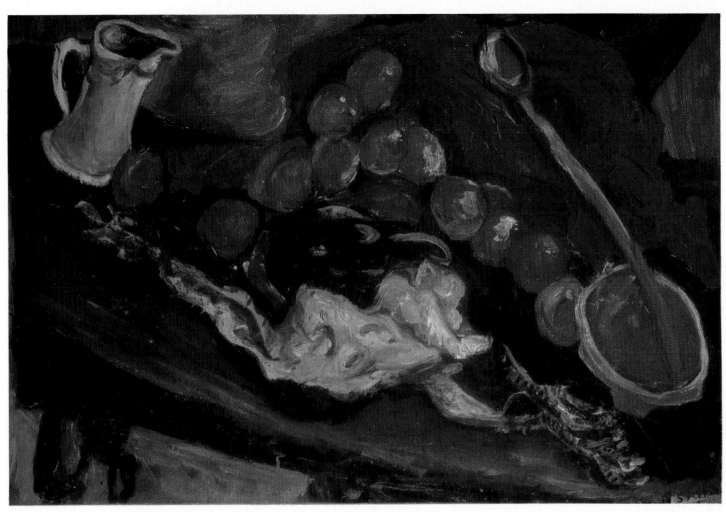

34

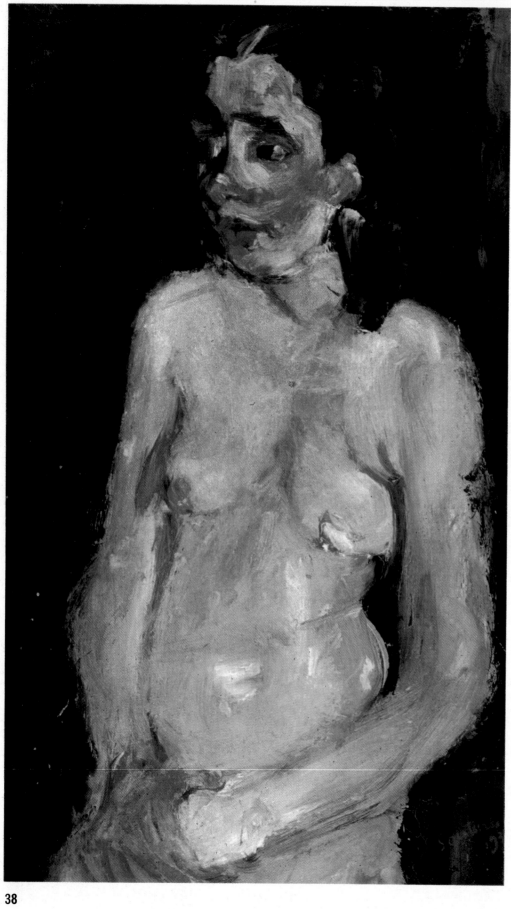

38

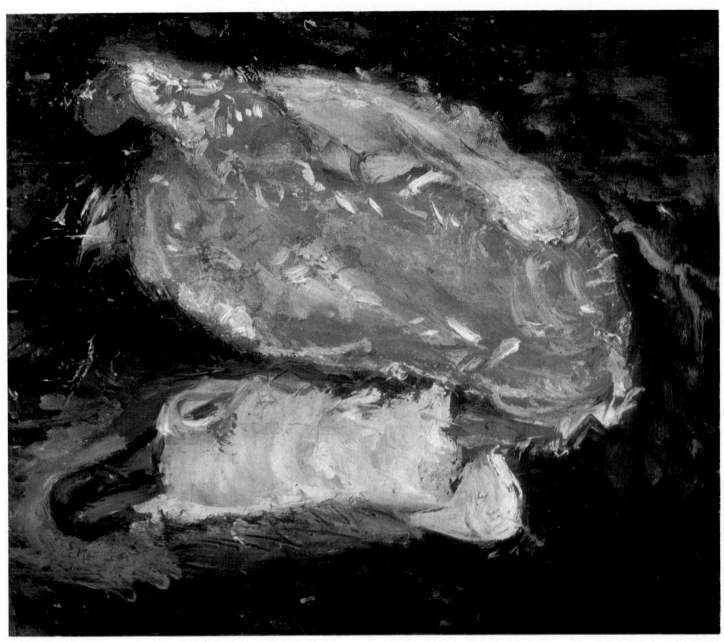

40

42

43

44

45

46

47

48